The Last Sunday in June
and
Other Plays

Other plays by Jonathan Tolins

The Unveiling

The Climate

Secrets of the Trade

One-Acts

The Man That Got Away

Stewart's Line

The Mid-Wife

Don't Look

JONATHAN TOLINS

The Last Sunday in June
and
Other Plays

Grove Press
New York

Published simultaneously in Canada
Printed in the United States of America

FIRST EDITION

Library of Congress Cataloging-in-Publication Data
Tolins, Jonathan.
      The last Sunday in June / by Jonathan Tolins.
          p. cm.
      ISBN 0-8021-4136-6
      1. Greenwich Village (New York, N.Y.)—Drama.   2. Gay couples—Drama.   3. Gay men—Drama.   I. Title.
      PS3570.O4275L37 2004
      812'.54—dc22   2003067755

Grove Press
841 Broadway
New York, NY 10003

04 05 06 07 08   10 9 8 7 6 5 4 3 2 1

Author's Note

On Gay Pride Day in 1997, some friends dropped by unannounced to watch the parade from my window. We joked about our gathering being the perfect setup for a "gay play" and riffed on some variations of the form. I thought the conversation was pretty entertaining, and so the next morning I wrote some of it down in a little blue notebook.

Thus began the shameless thievery that resulted in *The Last Sunday in June*. I am greatly indebted to my friends who were there that day and the many others who, over the next few years, shared their feelings, insights, and humor, all of which provided so much material for this play. (You know who you are.)

Once the script was complete, I continued to steal from many other talented people. Fortunately, in the theater this is known as "collaborating."

Ted Snowdon attended the first reading of the script, and from then on his enthusiasm and support never wavered. I couldn't ask for a more tenacious or sensitive producer. Not only did he get the play on, he made it better. Ted—along with David van Asselt at the Rattlestick Theater—pushed me to keep going deeper, and the play benefited greatly from their input.

I am indebted to all the actors and others who took part in readings and in the Genesius Guild workshop. And I am especially grateful to the brilliant Century Center/Rattlestick company under the always crisp direction of Trip Cullman. Trip and the cast mined every ounce of truth, humor, and pathos they could find in the script. Trip also showed me exactly where to cut. The pages that follow reflect these invaluable contributions.

The two earlier works in this collection went through similar gestations, and many talented people played a part; most, but not all, of them are listed in the credits that precede each play. Thank you to everyone who took part in the discussions, readings, and original productions of these plays. I must single out the wonderful directors, Arvin Brown and Leonard Foglia, who both taught me so much; and the brave producer, Charles Duggan, who single-handedly started my career.

Of course, there are agents and managers. The late Esther Sherman, Mark Subias, Michael Cardonick, Alan Gasmer, Jeff Field, and Peter Franklin all deserve mention. I must also thank my screenwriting partner, Seth Bass, who has been nothing but supportive of my time spent in the theater; and Eric Price at Grove/Atlantic for making this book a dream come true.

And finally, I want to thank my partner, Robert Cary, who improved my work in ways analogous to, but not equal to, the ways in which he improved my life.

CONTENTS

The Last Sunday in June   1

The Twilight of the Golds   103

If Memory Serves   199

THE LAST SUNDAY
IN JUNE

This play is dedicated to
Tom Campbell and Erick Neher

The Last Sunday in June opened at the Century Center for the Performing Arts (J. C. Compton, founder and director) on April 9, 2003. It was produced by Ted Snowdon with the following cast:

MICHAEL	Johnathan F. McClain
TOM	Peter Smith
JOE	David Turner
BRAD	Arnie Burton
CHARLES	Donald Corren
JAMES	Mark Setlock
SCOTT	Matthew Wilkas
SUSAN	Susan Pourfar

It was directed by Trip Cullman; the set design was by Takeshi Kata; the costume design was by Alejo Vietti; the lighting design was by Paul Whitaker; the sound design was by Jeffrey Yoshi Lee; and the casting was by Stephanie Klapper. The production manager was Kai Brothers; the general manager was Roy Gabay; and the associate producer was Morris Berchard. The production stage manager was Lori Ann Zepp.

The Last Sunday in June was originally produced in New York by the Rattlestick Theater (David Van Asselt, producing director; Sandra Coudert, managing director) in association with Ted Snowdon. It opened on February 9, 2003, with the cast and artistic staff listed above.

A workshop of this play, under its original title, *Another Gay Play,* was produced by the Genesius Guild (Thomas Morrissey, artistic director) in June of 2001, directed by the author.

The time: the last Sunday in June.

The setting: the living room in an apartment on Christopher Street in Greenwich Village. Though the room is not particularly spacious, the decor is attractive and comfortable, with the exception of two cheap lamps.

A decent-size New York City kitchen is on one side, upstage from the front door. It is immaculate, featuring the latest appliances and designer vinegar.

The other side of the stage is dominated by a window with a sill large enough for a person to sit, though not gracefully. A home office area, complete with computer, is in an alcove upstage, next to a door which leads to the bedroom and bathroom. Crowded bookshelves and a rather extensive CD collection line what little wall space is left.

At rise: MICHAEL, *thirty, is sitting in the window sill with a loose-leaf binder in his lap. He gazes absently through the open window at the street below. From outside, we hear the muted sounds of the Gay Pride parade—disco music, cheers, unintelligible speech through loudspeakers.*

After a moment, TOM, *Michael's lover, early thirties, calls out from the bedroom.*

TOM (*From offstage*)   What's happening out there?

MICHAEL   What?

TOM   What am I missing?

MICHAEL Lesbians. A whole lot of lesbians.

TOM What would you call that? A pack of lesbians? A gaggle?

MICHAEL I don't know. Maybe a loaf. A loaf of lesbians.

TOM That's good.

MICHAEL What are you doing?

TOM I'm deciding what to wear.

MICHAEL We're still going, right?

Tom enters, wearing khaki shorts and a bright green shirt.

TOM I said we were. Here, how's this?

MICHAEL That's what you're wearing?

TOM Fine, I'll change.

MICHAEL I'm kidding.

TOM (*Turning around*) Does my butt look too big?

MICHAEL What's "too big?"

TOM I'm serious.

MICHAEL It's perfect. One of those "bubble butts" we read about.

TOM Don't get me excited. What color belt?

MICHAEL Brown.

TOM So I look okay?

MICHAEL If you like green.

TOM I'm changing.

MICHAEL You're so ridiculous.

Tom returns to the bedroom.

TOM Like you never worry about how you look . . .

MICHAEL We're going to Pottery Barn to buy lamps.

TOM So? You look cute.

MICHAEL It's not a contest.

TOM Since when? And how do you think we get to Pottery Barn? We have to walk right through it just to cross the street. They're all down there, blocking our way.

MICHAEL Only if you let them.

Beat.

TOM What's happening now? What am I missing?

MICHAEL Nothing. The same.

TOM Loaves of lesbians?

MICHAEL More sapphic traffic.

TOM They're taking over, I swear.

MICHAEL They're better organized. And nicer. (*Sees something scary.*) Oh, God!

TOM What?

MICHAEL Topless!

Tom comes out and runs to the window. He's wearing a different shirt.

TOM Eew. Why do they have to do that?

MICHAEL They're fighting injustice. Why should they have to hide their tits when we don't?

TOM Because I don't want to look at them.

MICHAEL You're so anti-lesbian.

TOM I am not anti-lesbian. I just don't understand them.

MICHAEL They're way ahead of us.

TOM What does that mean?

MICHAEL It's not just about sex for them.

TOM (*Looking out the window*) Good thing.

The phone rings.

MICHAEL Are we going? You promised . . .

TOM Maybe it's too early to buy furniture. I don't want to jinx it; the house isn't officially ours yet.

MICHAEL I just want to look. And we need new lamps.

Tom picks up the cordless phone in the kitchen.

TOM Let me have my cereal.

MICHAEL Honey . . .

TOM (*Into phone*) Hello? Hi, Mom. Happy Gay Pride Day . . . Yeah, it's always the last Sunday in June. We're very proud. Aren't we, Mikey?

MICHAEL Practically bursting at the seams.

TOM (*Opening the refrigerator*) Nothing much. I went to the gym. (*To Michael.*) We're out of milk?

MICHAEL It went bad.

TOM (*Into phone*) Yeah, the parade finishes down our street. You should see it, it's a sea of rainbow flags down there.

MICHAEL I am so over the rainbow.

TOM It's inspiring. We're going to miss all this living in the sticks. No, there's no Gay Pride parade in Nyack.

MICHAEL   Thank God.

TOM   But Michael's right, we should get out of the city.

MICHAEL   What's left of it.

TOM   He did all the research, checking out neighborhoods, he's amazing . . . The deposit's already in. My hand was shaking when I wrote the check.

MICHAEL & TOM   It's a good investment.

TOM   The inspection's Tuesday. So, if all goes well . . .

MICHAEL   It will.

TOM   . . . this will be our last parade. We'll wave to you and Dad on TV. Watch for us. I'm going as a nun and Michael is dressed as Erin Brockovich.

MICHAEL   Why do you do that to her?

TOM   I'm kidding. Mom . . . We won't be on TV. Relax . . . No, we're going to Pottery Barn to buy lamps. See how well you raised me? I have no spirit left.

MICHAEL   (*Looking out the window*)   Thong.

TOM   (*As he runs to the window*)   I have to go. (*To Michael.*) Where? (*Into phone.*)   Ma, let me go, I'm busy.

MICHAEL   You can't see him anymore.

TOM   Shit. (*Into phone.*)   They're not going to fire me, half the firm is gay, partners too . . . Yes, Tom Hanks should have been so lucky. Okay, bye, Mom. That's all for today. I'm hanging up now. Bye. Bye-bye. Good-bye.

Tom hangs up.

MICHAEL   You're so mean to her.

TOM   We were done. Maybe I can see him from the bedroom. Did he go that way?

Tom runs to the bedroom.

MICHAEL   I don't know, maybe. He's not that great.

TOM (*From bedroom*)   I know, but the sheer idea of a thong on a Sunday morning. Wait, I think I . . . (*Unimpressed.*)   Oh, that guy. Yeah.

MICHAEL   I told you.

TOM   He shouldn't be wearing a thong.

MICHAEL   Let's face it, no one should.

TOM   Oh, I don't know. Some people can pull it off.

Tom appears in the doorway. He's changed his shirt again. His shorts are down around his ankles and his underwear is hiked up to look like a thong. He strikes a pose. Michael looks at him.

TOM (*cont.*)   Too much?

MICHAEL   So hot. Can we go now?

Tom smiles and approaches Michael, kissing the back of his neck and reaching down his undershirt.

TOM   Ooh, I love it when you call me hot.

MICHAEL   Tom, come on. I'm working. Cut it out.

TOM   What? I can't help myself. I'm a man possessed.

MICHAEL   You're stretching out the scoop.

TOM   I'll buy you a new one.

MICHAEL   You just get frisky after you've been to the gym.

Tom pulls away, hurt. He adjusts his underwear and pulls up his shorts.

TOM   Wow, that's a shitty thing to say.

MICHAEL   I can tell when you've been looking around in the sauna.

TOM   God, I was being affectionate. You looked so cute in the window . . . Forget it.

MICHAEL   Okay, you're right. I apologize. You can ravish me later.

TOM   You mean it?

MICHAEL   When we get back.

TOM   Excellent. Remind me.

MICHAEL   Will do. Now, let's go.

TOM   I thought you had work to do.

MICHAEL   I do. That's why I want to go shopping now and work later when it quiets down a little.

TOM   I haven't had my cereal. Let me just run down to the market and get some milk.

MICHAEL   Okay, I see where this is going.

TOM   What?

MICHAEL   If you don't want to go, just say so. I wouldn't mind if you would just come out and admit it.

TOM   We can go. It's just, it's Gay Pride. Our last one in the city. We should celebrate.

MICHAEL   Celebrate what?

The phone rings. Tom answers.

TOM   You're just brimming with self-hatred, aren't you?

MICHAEL   That's me.

TOM   (*Into phone*)   Hello? Joe! (*To Michael.*)   It's Joe.

MICHAEL   Say hi.

TOM   (*Into phone*)   Michael says hi. Happy Pride . . . Yeah, we can see the *homo*-stretch out the window . . . It just started . . . Well, we were supposed to go . . . Wait, hold on a sec . . . (*Covering the phone.*)   He asked if he could come over to watch the parade.

MICHAEL   When?

TOM   Now.

They stare at each other. They've negotiated these minor clashes of will countless times. Michael relents and gestures that anything's fine with him.

TOM   (*cont.*) (*Into phone*)   Sure, come over. We can walk through the festival thing . . . Now's good. I'm just running out to get milk but Michael's here . . . Okay, see you soon. Bye. (*Hangs up.*)   Sorry. I didn't feel like saying no. It makes sense, you can't see anything from the sidewalk . . .

MICHAEL   Whatever.

TOM   He won't stay long. We can go to Pottery Barn later . . .

MICHAEL   You know we won't. We'll be stuck here all day with ABBA and Gloria Gaynor wafting through the air.

TOM   So that's it.

MICHAEL   I hate Gay Pride Day. It makes me feel ugly and out-of-step. And mean.

TOM   You're not ugly. You're my cutie. Hi, cutie.

Tom snuggles up against Michael.

MICHAEL   Don't. I'm trying to stay mad.

TOM   You should be on one of those floats out there. The cutie float.

MICHAEL   My thong's at the cleaners.

Tom meows like a kitten. Michael doesn't respond. Tom meows again. Finally, Michael meows back.

TOM   I love you.

MICHAEL   Go buy your milk.

TOM   Be right back. Get your work done. We're going shopping later. (*Sexy . . .*)   And then . . .

MICHAEL   Don't get lost.

Tom exits, locking the door behind him. The noise from outside continues. Michael gets up and returns to the window, watching the scene, listening to the music. He glances back to the front door. Blackout.

SCENE TWO

Michael sits at the computer, using America Online. A glissando alerts him to an instant message. He reads it, then types one of his own. The sound of a key in the front door interrupts him. He quickly signs off. Tom enters the apartment with his carton of milk in a bag, just in time to hear the loud "good-bye" from the computer.

TOM   Caught you.

MICHAEL   You did not.

TOM   Getting a lot of work done, I see.

MICHAEL   I was just checking my mail.

TOM   Look who I found.

JOE, *late twenties, with a boyish smile and slight build, bursts into the room. Joe's enthusiasm and quirky energy make him seem younger than he is.*

JOE   Hi! Happy Pride!

Joe and Michael hug.

MICHAEL   Oh, God. Not you, too.

JOE   I got that from you guys. Ever since I heard Tom say it on the phone, I've been yelling "Happy Pride!" at people. The policemen love me!

TOM   Hey, how come I didn't get a hello hug?

JOE   Ooh, gosh, I don't know.

Tom hugs Joe closely and kisses him hello on the lips. Michael observes.

MICHAEL   Yay! Kissy-kissy, everybody's happy.

TOM   That's better. You want any cereal?

JOE   No thanks, I had a shake. I'm trying to bulk up.

TOM   Oh, Joe, don't even.

JOE   Please, no judgments. So, wow, you can see the parade from your window. That's so exciting!

MICHAEL   We can't believe our good fortune. We'll break out the poppers in a minute.

TOM   Don't listen to him.

MICHAEL   I'm self-hating.

JOE (*Looking out the window*)   You are? How interesting!

TOM   He's not self-hating; he just doesn't like gay men. You know what we did last night?

JOE   No, what?

TOM   We had dinner with a straight couple in Brooklyn. Can you imagine?

MICHAEL   Another teacher, Sherry, and her husband. Very sweet people.

TOM   Only my boyfriend would set up a straight dinner *in Brooklyn* on Gay Pride weekend. And you should have seen him walking home from the subway, eyes fixed straight ahead, not looking at anything or anybody. Like Scarlett O'Hara marching through the wounded of Atlanta.

MICHAEL   That is not true.

TOM   "As God is my witness, I'll never be horny again!"

MICHAEL   I was tired.

JOE   I understand, it can be overwhelming. God, look at all those pecs! It's so hard to pick favorites. To pick a peck of pecs . . . Oh my God, I think I just wrote a new Sondheim song. (*To Michael.*)   What are you working on?

MICHAEL   Lesson plans for the fall. I'm up for a job near our new house.

TOM   It's not "our house" yet. Barry said . . .

JOE   Who's Barry?

TOM The real estate broker. He said don't count your chickens. We have to wait for the inspection, finish up with the bank . . .

MICHAEL Tom's getting cold feet.

TOM I am not. It's just a very big investment.

MICHAEL Which we can afford.

TOM Said the school teacher to the attorney.

JOE So did you have an interview in the principal's office?

MICHAEL So far so good.

TOM They love him. He's an amazing teacher.

JOE And the school is cool about everything?

MICHAEL You mean my "secret life?" It's a private school; they prefer it.

JOE I can't believe you're moving to the suburbs, surrounded by all those straight people. Won't you be nervous around your neighbors?

TOM Which ones? The antique dealers or the ex–chorus boys?

MICHAEL They keep to themselves and their yards are immaculate.

JOE Wow. Did you ever think, when you first met, this would be the person you would be with forever?

MICHAEL No way.

TOM I did.

MICHAEL You did not.

TOM Well, I kind of did. (*To Joe.*) He was temping at my firm when I was an intern.

MICHAEL I was on summer break and needed the money.

TOM And from my desk, I could stare at the back of his head.

MICHAEL I had no idea. I was playing Tetris.

TOM Then one day a bunch of us went out to lunch. Michael didn't talk much, but everything he said was devastating. He was the funniest one at the table.

MICHAEL They were all lawyers.

TOM I knew right away, this person would be important to me.

JOE What about you?

MICHAEL It took me a little longer. He made me dinner one night here in the apartment. And after we ate, he sat me down and played me his favorite opera and show CDs.

TOM He fell asleep, which I thought was cute at the time.

MICHAEL But he was so sweet, like a little kid, showing his prized possessions. I remember thinking, "This is a good guy. He'd be nice to come home to."

They kiss.

JOE That is so romantic. And such a good meeting story. Most gay couples just say, "We met at a party," because they really met online in Men for Men Boxer Briefs *Now!*

TOM (*Singing like Chevalier*) "Ah, yes, I remember it well."

JOE I'm so happy for you guys. You two are showing the world that gay people are really grounded. (*Looking out the window.*) There's a guy in overalls, no shirt. I love that.

MICHAEL   Homo on the range.

The phone rings. Tom answers.

JOE   He's so cute! He's just like a real farm boy . . . who's been to an electrolysist.

TOM   (*Into phone*)   Hello? No, this is Tom. I can't hear you . . . oh, hi, Charles. Sure, come over. (*He hangs up.*)   That was Charles on his cell phone. He's coming over.

MICHAEL   Great. The more the merrier.

TOM   Come on, don't be that way.

JOE   Wait. What am I missing? Who's Charles?

MICHAEL   One of Tom's opera friends.

TOM   He manages opera singers. I need someone to go with me who doesn't fall asleep. You'll like Charles, he's smart. Older. He should add some perspective to the day, which some of us seem to need.

JOE   You don't like him?

MICHAEL   He's fine.

TOM   Michael's just in a mood because we're not at Pottery Barn.

JOE   Ooh, Pottery Barn, I love the way they smell. What do you need?

MICHAEL   Stuff for the house. And we need to replace those lamps. They scream "dorm room."

JOE   They look good to me. But I love this apartment.

TOM   It starts showing this week.

JOE   I wish. Nope, I'm stuck in my tiny hovel. It's amazing what most New Yorkers put up with.

MICHAEL   Then why did you leave L.A.?

JOE   It's too spread out.

The intercom buzzes. Tom presses the button to open the front door.

TOM   That was fast.

JOE   And I'm more attractive here.

MICHAEL   (*Dubious*)   Really.

JOE   Totally. First of all, I look better in layers of clothing. And in New York, there aren't all these chiseled, perfect-body freaks.

MICHAEL   Really.

JOE   Well, all right, there are, but they're not all actors.

TOM   Joe, *you're* an actor.

JOE   Yeah, but I don't sound like one.

TOM   That's what counts.

JOE   And they're not the guys I find most attractive anyway. I like those guys in suits on the subway coming home from work, with five-o'clock shadow, you know. (*He growls like Eartha Kitt.*)   They just have this "*real*" thing that's so sexy. It drives me crazy. And they're approachable, you feel like you have a chance. You don't have to be perfect.

TOM   Then why are you trying to "bulk up"?

JOE   That's for health reasons.

MICHAEL   Really.

JOE It's true. I'm doing it on the advice of my trainer . . .

The doorbell rings.

JOE (*cont.*)   . . . who is completely certified.

Tom opens the door. BRAD, mid-thirties, enters. There's a restless energy about Brad that has its origin in intense need. He wears strands of rainbow-colored plastic beads around his neck.

TOM Brad! What are you doing here?

BRAD Well, when you ask it that way, I'm not so sure myself.

He turns dramatically and walks away.

TOM Get back here.

BRAD (*Walking right in*)   Okay.

Tom kisses Brad on the lips.

TOM It's good to see you.

BRAD I was in the neighborhood. There seems to be some kind of street fair going on. I bought these lovely beads so as not to offend the natives.

Brad puts a strand of beads around Tom's neck.

TOM You're so fun. You're the king of fun.

BRAD What does that make you?

MICHAEL The king of patronizing our guests. Hi, Brad.

Michael hugs Brad. Brad puts another strand of beads around Michael's neck.

BRAD One for you.

MICHAEL They match my charm bracelet. You!

Michael returns to the window sill.

TOM   Brad, you know Joe, don't you?

BRAD   Yes, I do. Do I?

JOE   We've met, but you wouldn't remember.

BRAD   When?

JOE   When you came to school to visit Tom after you graduated. I was a freshman.

BRAD   That would make you . . .

TOM   Much younger than you.

Brad laughs and pulls the sides of his face back with his hands, giving himself instant plastic surgery.

BRAD   Yes, but no one would believe it.

JOE   I met you at a party. You gave me this whole lecture about Whitney Houston.

BRAD   Which one?

JOE   The singer.

BRAD   No, which lecture?

JOE   Oh, you said that even if she never did anything else of value, she made a lasting contribution to American culture with her Diet Coke commercial.

BRAD   Very true. Brilliant use of a woman who can't dance. And it's been downhill ever since. But, I'm sorry, that doesn't help me remember you. Do you have any idea how many times I delivered that sermon?

TOM   It was always a favorite.

BRAD   Thank you. See, that's what Gay Pride Day is all about.

23

JOE Friendship?

BRAD No. It reminds us that if I had a great body, I wouldn't have to be so fucking charming.

MICHAEL Are you fishing? Is he fishing?

TOM You're very attractive, Brad.

BRAD Sure.

The intercom Buzzes. Tom presses the button.

TOM That's Charles.

BRAD (*Spoken, acted to the hilt*) Mother always said I'd be very attractive when I grew up. *When I grew up!* "Different," she said. "With a special something and a very very personal flair. And though I was eight or nine . . ."

TOM "Though you were eight or nine . . ."

MICHAEL "Though you were eight or nine . . ."

JOE (*Sings, triumphant*) "You hated her!"

Tom, Michael, and Brad look at Joe, impressed.

JOE (*cont.*) I did *Chorus Line* in summer stock.

BRAD Sheila or Val?

JOE Butch.

BRAD This is going to be a good day.

The doorbell rings. Tom opens the door for CHARLES, fifty. He has the fussy and slightly impatient manner of a middle-aged gay man who lives alone.

CHARLES Have you been out there? It's amazing. In twenty-five years absolutely everything about gay life has changed except the Gay Pride parade.

TOM   Hello, Charles.

Tom does not kiss Charles. There's an awkward bit of arm touching.

CHARLES   Who are all these people? I didn't know I'd have to deal with all these new people.

TOM   Don't panic. Charles, this is Brad and Joe.

CHARLES   That tells me very little.

TOM   Joe is an actor and Brad writes for *Entertainment Weekly*.

JOE   I didn't know that.

TOM   And, of course, you remember Michael.

MICHAEL   Hi, Charles.

CHARLES   Hello. Wait! Look at you, sitting there in the window. You look like you're in a play.

TOM   What . . . ?

The others step downstage and look up at Michael. He poses for effect.

JOE   Oh, my God, you do. With the parade out the window. (*Sings.*)   "Before the parade passes by . . ."

CHARLES   Not that play.

TOM   It does look like a stage set from here.

BRAD   I wouldn't know. I don't cover theater.

CHARLES   It could be a gay play. About gays on Gay Pride Day.

MICHAEL   Just what we need, another gay play.

CHARLES   Don't knock gay theater. It's very important historically. It used to be the only way we could see ourselves.

BRAD   Well, now we're "Must-See TV," so get over it.

TOM (*Taking out a Playbill*)   Exactly. If I have to sit through one more gay play, I'll scream. We just saw this one.

CHARLES (*Reading the Playbill*)   *Curious George: Adventures of a Reel Fag*, spelled *R-E-E-L.*

JOE   Oh, I saw a poster for that. What's it about?

TOM   George Cukor and his life as a gay director in Hollywood.

CHARLES   That sounds interesting.

MICHAEL   You'd think.

JOE   Wait. Then how come the poster is six guys in Speedos?

TOM   Pool party.

BRAD   Is that on the cover? Give me that.

He takes the Playbill and examines the picture, panting lewdly.

TOM   You see? That's how they try to lure us in. It's disgusting.

MICHAEL   We went.

CHARLES   But that's not really a gay play.

MICHAEL   Could have fooled me.

CHARLES   No, a gay play is one with a bunch of gay guys in an apartment or a country house bitching and cracking jokes about what it means to be gay.

BRAD   That would never happen.

CHARLES   And all the characters are witty and touching as they laugh through the pain of being reviled. That's a gay play.

TOM   I hate classifying everything that way. "Gay play." What's a "straight play"?

MICHAEL   Mamet.

CHARLES   You see? That's exactly the kind of joke that would be in the play about us.

TOM   This is getting creepy.

JOE   Oh, and then we'd play a truth game and reveal ugly secrets about each other!

MICHAEL   Let's not.

BRAD   And the losers would have to get naked. (*Mimes taking off his shirt.*)   "You guys! What? Not my pants too! Oh, okay." (*Mimes taking off his pants.*)   "What? Not my underwear! I'm going to get you guys for this, I swear!" (*Mimes wriggling out of his underwear.*)   "What? I don't really have to bend over and expose my sphincter, do I? You guys!"

EVERYBODY ELSE (*Various ad-lib*)   Stop! We get it. You're grossing me out!

CHARLES   And then we'd do a dance. Curtain. End of act one.

JOE   Oh, and then in act two, it's Gay Pride Day a year later, and one of us is gone. But we don't say anything about it for like twenty minutes. Then someone breaks down and we all hug.

CHARLES   Yes! Exactly, that's exactly right!

TOM   All right, that's enough. I don't like this game.

CHARLES   Why not? It's so postmodern.

JOE It's very "meta."

TOM I just think we should stop. Just stop, okay?

CHARLES What, have we said something . . . ?

MICHAEL Hey, didn't you guys want to watch the parade?

CHARLES Ooh, right, I have to be on the lookout.

TOM For what?

CHARLES (*Taking out a Pride guide*) For a boyfriend, what else? It's what today is for. I can't even count how many relationships I've had that began on Gay Pride Day.

MICHAEL How long did they last?

CHARLES That would depend on his summer share. Let's see what we're up to, I have a program. The key is being on the street at the right time . . . (*Checking the program.*) Have we seen Dykes on Bikes?

At that moment, the roar of motorcycles is heard from outside.

CHARLES (*cont.*) Okay, next is the Athletic-slash-Leather contingent.

Joe rushes to the window. Charles follows. Michael is still sitting there, however.

JOE I love "slash" anything.

CHARLES Well, we can't all fit here, can we?

TOM You know, you can see more from the bedroom.

CHARLES (*To Joe*) Shall we?

JOE Oh. Sure.

They head off together.

CHARLES   So, you're an actor?

JOE   Yes, but I don't sound like one.

They're gone. Beat.

TOM   Sorry about that.

BRAD   Don't worry about it.

TOM   Joe's still young. He doesn't think . . . He figures we're all too young to be . . .

MICHAEL   Tom, leave it alone.

BRAD   It's okay, really. AIDS is over. Andrew Sullivan said so in the *Times*.

MICHAEL   How are you doing, Brad? Everything good?

BRAD   Fine. That's the only hard part now, deciding who to tell. It's like I'm back in the closet. It makes me tense.

TOM   I can imagine.

MICHAEL   No you can't.

Tom and Brad move to the kitchen. Michael joins them.

BRAD   The other day, this kid, this punk, sat across from me on the subway. He was wearing his pants belted down by his knees—they always wear a long jacket so I can't tell where their crotch is; it's like a homoerotic Escher print—anyway, he's sitting there looking at me. And he takes out a knife. A really big knife.

MICHAEL   Oh, God.

BRAD   Our eyes meet. And he says, "Am I scaring you?" And I said, "I take thirty-one pills a day. Nothing scares me."

TOM   Then what happened?

BRAD   Nothing. He laughed. He left me alone.

Brad opens the refrigerator and pulls out a can of Diet Coke. He then takes a small pill case from his bag.

TOM   You shouldn't do things like that. You have to be careful.

BRAD   Too late. So he's cute, what's–his–name.

TOM   Joe.

BRAD   Very cute. What's his story?

TOM   He's recently out. Not that there was ever a question. But now it's official.

MICHAEL   And he's making up for lost time.

TOM   He's very enthusiastic.

MICHAEL   And indiscriminate.

BRAD   I like that!

TOM   He's at that stage where he finds everyone he meets fascinating.

BRAD   (*Gesturing to the bedroom*)   Oh, that explains . . . (*Doing his impression of a toothless old man, complete with walker.*)   I'm going to go see the parade!

TOM   Charles is smart and funny. And still attractive.

BRAD   And I'm . . . hello?!

MICHAEL   It's not a contest.

BRAD   Since when?

Brad takes pills with a sip of Diet Coke. He holds up the can and speaks like a fashion model . . .

BRAD (*cont.*)   Ooh. I'm so full. This was almost a calorie.

Brad pulls a protein bar from his bag and eats it.

TOM   Well, anyway, I apologize. I'll tell Joe to be more careful about what he says.

BRAD   No . . . Don't.

TOM   Okay.

MICHAEL   Do you really take thirty-one pills a day?

BRAD   If you count Ambien, Paxil, and Altoids.

Charles and Joe emerge from the bedroom in conversation. Charles is holding a large pair of opera glasses.

JOE   That is so true what you say about nipples.

CHARLES   Isn't it?

TOM   What are you talking about?

CHARLES   Small talk. I found these in your dresser.

JOE   Why have you all moved to the kitchen? You're telling secrets!

TOM   No. (*Covering.*)   We were about to show Brad our new juicer.

JOE   Wow. Can we see, too?

Tom brings out a huge juicer. It hits the counter with a thud.

TOM   Here she is.

CHARLES   You must really like juice.

TOM This thing's amazing. You don't have to peel an orange—just throw it in.

CHARLES Isn't that unsanitary?

TOM You wash it first. It's like an outboard motor in there. You could get juice from a brick.

Tom turns it on. The roar of the motor is deafening. Tom turns it off.

MICHAEL You see what I have to live with?

TOM (*Looking in the refrigerator*) We're out of everything juiceable.

MICHAEL You went to the store.

TOM I didn't know.

JOE Hey, you know this could be a great prop in the play. Like any time there's an awkward pause . . .

CHARLES Right, or if someone lies.

JOE Yes! Like a lie detector. That would be so funny. Wouldn't that be funny?

BRAD Hilarious.

Brad punctuates his line with a roar from the juicer.

TOM Can we stop with the play thing? It's freaking me out. And this is not a toy.

BRAD Sorry.

JOE It is a beautiful juicer. You guys have the perfect life.

CHARLES So why don't you two get married?

TOM We're not allowed.

CHARLES You know what I mean.

JOE A commitment ceremony!

BRAD A circle jerk, something.

MICHAEL I'd feel silly. If it's not the real thing . . .

TOM The ceremony or the relationship?

MICHAEL Which do you think I meant?

BRAD I hate it when they get like this. (*Covering his ears and singing.*) La la la la la la la . . .

CHARLES You should at least exchange rings. It could be beautiful, and covered in the Style section in the *Times*. Two men decked out in Armani, standing under a floral *chuppah,* the band playing "Sunrise Sunset." A room at Tavern on the Green, with specially commissioned topiaries depicting scenes from the lyric stage . . .

MICHAEL You've thought about this before.

CHARLES If I was with someone now, I'd want a ceremony. And a ring.

TOM We just don't feel the need for some imitation public ritual. We reject straight middle-class values.

Another roar from the juicer. Brad pretends it was an accident.

TOM (*cont.*) Cut that out.

BRAD Are there any other kitchen appliances you want to show us before you move to the suburbs, you transgender revolutionaries?

TOM You've made your point.

MICHAEL Face it, sweetie, we're pathetic fuddy-duddies.

TOM   Maybe we're post-gay.

BRAD   Or straight.

JOE   Do you think you'll ever have kids?

TOM   We'd like to but we're putting it off.

JOE   Till when?

MICHAEL   Till it's too late.

CHARLES   Well, more power to you, whatever you do. Cling to each other. Believe me, cruising in your forties is a real drag.

BRAD   What about in your fifties?

CHARLES   Fuck you.

BRAD   Sorry, I like younger guys.

CHARLES   See what I mean?

JOE   Okay, but cruising in your twenties is a blast.

CHARLES   Is he charming or insensitive?

MICHAEL   The jury's still out.

JOE   I'm sure I'll grow out of it.

BRAD   Not necessarily.

JOE   But right now, it's such a thrill. Walking down Eighth Avenue, seeing somebody cute, catching their eye, following them a block or two . . .

BRAD   Or forty. (*Off everyone's look.*)   Oh, like I'm the only stalker.

JOE   It's exciting. Even when it doesn't lead to sex.

MICHAEL   Really.

BRAD That's true. I figured that out when my sister came to visit. I'd cruise a guy, he'd cruise me back, but I couldn't do anything because my fucking sister was there. But then I learned to appreciate the moment, what we gave each other. "You're cute, you think I'm cute. I don't have to sleep with you. Just thanks for the fantasy, I'll be on my way."

TOM That's very healthy.

JOE And what is sex nowadays anyway? It's just you rub me, I rub you, wait, I'll get a towel.

CHARLES Sounds good to me.

BRAD (*Taking the opera glasses*) Can I borrow these?

JOE It's those brief moments of heat that get me. You know, a look, a smile. You guys must miss that sometimes.

Tom and Michael look to each other.

BRAD (*Searching with opera glasses*) Oh, hello. Look at these two.

CHARLES What?

BRAD These two guys, no shirts, walking hand in hand down the center of the street. Luscious.

CHARLES (*Looking, with a gasp*) Oh, my God, they're spectacular. They're not carrying a sign or anything. They're their own float.

MICHAEL What is that about?

TOM It's about, "Eat your heart out, scrawny losers."

JOE Maybe it's the one day of the year they can hold hands.

They all turn and look at Joe.

CHARLES Will you marry me?

BRAD I saw him first.

JOE I'm really not ready to make a commitment.

BRAD In that case . . . (*Instantly back to the window.*) Where are they?

TOM Anyone who can spend that much time at the gym can't be very interesting.

BRAD Keep telling yourself that.

MICHAEL I hate the gym. I wear a yarmulke.

JOE What?

MICHAEL Our gym is a meat market, so I wear a yarmulke. No one wants to cruise an Orthodox Jew. It just isn't sexy.

CHARLES Things are so different now. It's the steroids. Those guys don't have to spend as much time working out because of the drugs.

JOE I saw a guy at the gym sticking a needle in his ass in the locker room. I didn't find it attractive.

CHARLES You know what else has changed? How unfriendly and rude they are.

TOM I hate this. Who's "they"?

CHARLES The body guys.

TOM What does that make us?

MICHAEL The ones who wear sleeves.

CHARLES They used to be much more open; everybody knew some of them. Now they're this closed society. You can't get near them, let alone sleep with them.

BRAD   Not true. Sorry, but it can be done. All it takes is a little determination and a lack of pride.

TOM   "With an emphasis on the latter."

Tom goes to the CD collection to find his Damn Yankees *recordings.*

CHARLES   But we're not friends with them. Not anymore.

JOE   God, how depressing. But wait, Tom, what about that guy you were talking to outside the grocery store?

TOM   What?

BRAD   Who was that?

MICHAEL   Yes. Who was that?

TOM   Who are you . . . oh, oh, Scott.

MICHAEL   Who's Scott?

TOM   You remember. I met him when I was doing pro bono work for that hospice?

JOE   He's incredible.

TOM   Thank you, Joe.

MICHAEL   Funny, I've never met him.

TOM   I've told you about him.

MICHAEL   That's not the same thing.

BRAD   Tension. (*Covering his ears and singing.*)   La la la la la la la.

TOM   Oh, please, you're not really jealous.

MICHAEL   I don't know, should I be?

TOM   Well, you'll find out soon enough. I invited him to stop by if he feels like it.

JOE   Oh, my God!

BRAD   I need to shave everything.

CHARLES   He won't come. Those guys never come.

BRAD   Again not true.

MICHAEL   Well, nice of you to tell me.

TOM   Oh, don't be that way.

MICHAEL   I just find it very interesting, the way you have your secret boyfriends.

TOM   Oh, please. If I wanted to keep him secret, would I invite him over?

CHARLES   You would if you were sure he wouldn't come.

TOM   Thank you, Charles.

JOE   I'm sorry I brought him up. He wasn't *that* cute. And I only saw him from far away.

TOM   He's a friend. Not even.

MICHAEL   Whatever. It's fine.

CHARLES   Boy, do you see that? This guy isn't even here and look what happens. It's amazing, the power they have over us.

BRAD   (*Looking out the window*)   Every ripple.

TOM   Each "scintilla of basket."

MICHAEL   (*Laughing*)   Oh, God.

JOE   What is that?

TOM   It's from a novel by this guy we know . . . Brad, it's from *Circuit Boy*.

Tom finds the book on a shelf and searches for the passage.

BRAD What's that?

TOM James's novel.

BRAD Oh. I never read it.

TOM You never read it? You dated him for a month.

BRAD I read the jacket.

TOM Doesn't *Entertainment Weekly* cover books?

BRAD Don't get snippy. You dated him a lot longer than I did.

JOE You did?

TOM A year or something.

BRAD In college, that's forever.

TOM Yeah, well, *I* read the book.

BRAD I spent a whole month listening to him cry over you. Fucking drama queen . . .

TOM Here it is, listen to this. "I stepped inside the dungeon-like bar and was bombarded by those familiar sights, sounds, and smells. Stale beer, a Madonna dance mix, and guys. Guys and guys and guys and guys and guys and guys. (*Turns the page.*) "And guys and guys and guys and guys."

CHARLES Does it really say that?

TOM "Without conscious command, my eyes scanned this evening's panoply for every sharp jaw, every blue eye, every curvy ass, every sign of youth and sex that fit my type of the moment, as changeable as my Chelsea-boy haircut. And as cheap."

JOE   This is embarrassing.

MICHAEL   Wait.

TOM   "Searching, searching, never in vain. My personal Geiger counter throbs and buzzes as it nears its quarry, responding to each glimpse of possibility, each scintilla of basket."

MICHAEL   We love that phrase.

CHARLES   It's a bit much.

JOE (*To Brad and Tom*)   You guys dated this person?

MICHAEL   Yup.

TOM   James is a great guy. He's smart and sensitive.

BRAD   That's an understatement.

TOM   He could be a lot of fun, sometimes.

CHARLES   I remember when the book came out. It wasn't a hit.

TOM   It was panned.

MICHAEL   I read it. I didn't get much out of it.

BRAD   Maybe you should put it in the juicer.

JOE   How often do you see this guy?

TOM   Not for a while.

MICHAEL   Thank God.

TOM   When the book came out . . . it was awkward; he could tell we didn't like it.

BRAD   I saw him last year at the White Party, working very hard. I ducked behind a leather daddy.

TOM   It's terrible, the way we lose touch. I'm going to call him.

MICHAEL   Now?

TOM (*Checking his address book*)   I'll invite him over.

JOE   I want to go back down. I'm getting antsy. I think it's time.

TOM (*Dialing*)   We'll go. Don't worry, he won't be home.

MICHAEL   You always have to be everybody's friend.

TOM   What's wrong with that?

BRAD (*At the window*)   Here comes the mayor.

Charles runs to the window.

CHARLES   Boo! Boo! Come on, everybody, it's tradition. Boo!

Brad and Joe boo along with Charles.

BRAD   Why are we booing?

CHARLES   The gay thing.

JOE   Which gay thing?

CHARLES   I don't know, but there's always some gay thing.

They boo.

TOM   Quiet, I got his machine.

They boo more quietly.

TOM (*cont.*) (*Into phone*)   Hey, James, it's Tom. Blast from the past. I'm sorry about that. Anyway, I was thinking about you, it being Gay Pride. There are a bunch of us down here watching the parade. Michael . . .

BRAD (*Sotto voce*)   Don't tell him I'm . . .

TOM   Brad. I'd love to hear from you. I'm sure you're out in the thick of it, so to speak, but if you want to stop by or call, that'd be great. I miss you. Okay, bye.

MICHAEL   Got a little mushy with your ex there, don't you think?

TOM   I feel bad. He was a good friend.

MICHAEL (*Affectionate*)   I know. You're very sweet.

JOE   Well, if nobody's coming, I think we should go out.

CHARLES   Yes, I could use another dose.

BRAD   I've started to feel good about myself; it's time to nip that in the bud.

JOE   You guys coming?

TOM   Sure. I can get some things to juice. Michael?

MICHAEL   I need to work.

TOM   You sure you can't just . . . okay.

JOE   If that guy Scott comes, don't let him leave.

MICHAEL   I'll use my wily ways.

JOE   This will be fun.

BRAD (*His arm around Joe as they go*)   Okay, so we covered Whitney. Let's move on to Olivia.

CHARLES   De Havilland?

Brad and Joe exit with Charles on their heels. Tom lingers at the door and meows at Michael. Michael hisses back. Blackout.

SCENE THREE

Michael waits with JAMES, *early thirties. The conversation has just reached an awkward lull.*

MICHAEL   You're sure you don't want anything?

JAMES   No. Thanks. It's funny, on the intercom, I thought you were Tom.

MICHAEL   We get that a lot. When we go out, people always think we're brothers. It's a little unsettling.

JAMES   I guess gay men try so hard to look the same . . .

MICHAEL   I think it's just something that happens after you live together for a while. It happens to heterosexual couples, but they've still got the gender difference to keep things straight.

JAMES   As it were.

MICHAEL   This woman at a museum once asked if we were twins. Bizarre. Tom thinks they just don't know how to process two average-looking men being that close and easy with each other. So they decide we must be brothers. It's stupid.

JAMES   That's a little dismissive of straight people, don't you think? Maybe you two do look alike. Or maybe it has something to do with gay narcissism; you were both attracted to someone who reminded you of yourself.

Beat. Michael decides to let it go.

MICHAEL   They just went to get some food and look around. They should be back any minute.

JAMES   It's a little odd, don't you think?

MICHAEL What is?

JAMES Tom invites me over after all this time and then leaves.

MICHAEL Oh, well, I guess he figured you were out, enjoying the festivities.

JAMES God, is that possible?

MICHAEL Is what possible?

JAMES To enjoy the festivities.

MICHAEL Some people like it. It's comforting, I guess—the chance to see how many of us there are. "No one is alone."

JAMES Then why aren't you outside?

MICHAEL It's not my thing.

JAMES Good for you.

James smiles at Michael. The moment is too weird for either of them. Michael turns away.

JAMES (*cont.*) I was pretty surprised when I picked up my messages. What made Tom call me out of the blue?

MICHAEL I don't know, we were talking . . . Your book came up in the conversation.

JAMES *Circuit Boy?* How? How did it come up?

MICHAEL (*Thinks, then*) I don't remember.

JAMES Oh come on. Think. Who mentioned it first?

MICHAEL You ask a lot of questions.

JAMES Are you sure?

MICHAEL   Yes, you do.

JAMES   No, are you sure you don't remember?

MICHAEL   Oh . . . I think Tom saw it on the shelf, it caught his eye. That's it.

James sees the book and picks it up, looks at the jacket, flips the pages.

JAMES   God, here it is. I hate that picture. It's weird, I don't even feel like I wrote this anymore. I'm such a different person now.

MICHAEL   It wasn't that long ago.

JAMES   (*Smiling, mysterious*)   No. I guess not.

Tom opens the front door with his key, still in conversation with Brad, who enters right behind.

TOM   But why is it called "Gay Pride"? Shouldn't it be "Gay Contentment"?

BRAD   Pride is easier.

TOM   (*Spotting James*)   James. God, hi.

Tom hugs James.

JAMES   Hello, Tom.

TOM   How long have you been here?

JAMES   Ten minutes? I think I've been bothering your boyfriend.

MICHAEL   Don't be silly.

Behind James's back, Michael makes a face to convey just how excruciating his time with James has been.

JAMES Hello, Brad.

BRAD I'm sorry, have we met? I'm kidding! It's good to see you. How are you?

JAMES I'm great. Finally.

BRAD (*Whatever*) Okay.

MICHAEL What happened to the others?

TOM They took the stairs. Something about leg muscles.

BRAD I figure the old guy will talk himself out and then I go in for the kill.

TOM Brad, shhh!

Charles and Joe enter, in conversation.

JOE So no matter what line of work you're in, you can still have good calves.

CHARLES I've found that to be true.

TOM Charles, Joe, this is James.

JOE Oh, hi.

JAMES Hello.

CHARLES I remember when your book came out.

JAMES Did you read it?

CHARLES No, and you really shouldn't ask that of people.

JAMES It's all right. I'm glad you didn't.

TOM (*Putting away groceries*) Don't say that. I liked it a lot.

JAMES Let's not start this again.

46

TOM   I didn't agree with all of it, but there are some wonderful passages in there. The reviews were very unfair.

MICHAEL (*Changing the subject*)   So how was it outside?

JOE   It was great!

CHARLES   It's ridiculous. Ten blocks of booths selling fried, greasy food that nobody has the nerve to eat.

JAMES   Typical.

JOE   I saw my trainer.

BRAD   And I saw a prostitute . . . (*Off everyone's look.*)   who I've met.

JAMES   Were they the same guy?

JOE   If only.

BRAD   Trainers and prostitutes—variations on a theme. Beautiful men paid to touch you.

CHARLES   There's a difference. Prostitutes get results.

JAMES   Whatever they do, they make us feel like shit. My hairdresser's the same way.

BRAD   Not mine. Mine kisses me on the lips and wears crop tops. You have to love anyone who spends his entire day in front of a mirror.

JAMES   I don't.

BRAD   Oh, and I also saw the question guy.

MICHAEL   Who?

BRAD   That guy I went on a date with who wouldn't stop asking questions.

CHARLES Was that when you told us to walk faster?

BRAD Yes. Asshole.

JAMES Michael accused me of asking too many questions before you got here.

MICHAEL I didn't *accuse* . . .

JAMES I guess you guys don't like having to explain anything.

BRAD After "cut" or "uncut," what's left to say?

JOE So what did this guy ask you?

BRAD First and only date, we sit down for drinks and he asks how much I make, do I hate my parents, what I like sexually . . .

JOE Eeew.

BRAD I go along with it, I can hold my own. Then he cuts to final Jeopardy, his big litmus test: "If you could change one person's mind in all of history, whose would it be?"

JOE I would have said mine, for coming on this date.

MICHAEL And your answer was?

BRAD Diana Ross, so she'd never leave the Supremes.

TOM Great answer.

JOE Oh my God, that's perfect.

JAMES You think so?

BRAD I mean, okay, okay, I know, *Hitler*. But a lot of good things came out of World War Two. People came together, women wore snoods. Whereas my life would have been affected much more deeply if the Supremes had held on for a few more hits.

CHARLES   So what happened?

BRAD   She went off and made *Mahogany*.

CHARLES   On the date.

BRAD   Then it was my turn. So I asked my standard American history question.

TOM   Which is?

BRAD   "If you could sleep with anyone involved in the O. J. Simpson trial, who would it be?" He said Kato Kaelin. It was over.

MICHAEL   Right. You don't want to date a Kato lover.

JOE   I don't know, I liked Kato.

TOM   We all liked Kato a little, but not first choice.

CHARLES   Yes, Kato is an obvious, pedestrian answer.

TOM   Give me Allan Park, the limo driver.

JOE   Oh, I remember him, he was adorable.

MICHAEL   The DNA lawyer with the bushy hair . . .

TOM   Barry Scheck.

BRAD   Cute, but you don't want to see him naked.

MICHAEL   What about O. J.? Remember those pictures at the police station of him in his gray underwear?

TOM   You're sleeping on the couch tonight.

JOE   Brad, who did you pick?

BRAD   No contest. Fuhrman.

CHARLES   Fuhrman! Yes!

BRAD   Okay, okay, I know he's a racist. But the man was sexy, and that was not diminished by his repeated use of the *n* word.

CHARLES   (*Swooning for effect*)   I think it helped. That military hair, the nasty expression, those pictures in *Vanity Fair* with the pickup truck. I just wanted him to interrogate me with a hose. I'll say anything, just get the hose!

Tom, Michael, Brad, and Joe laugh and cheer for Charles until . . .

JAMES   Jesus, what the fuck is wrong with all of you? Two people died. Do you have to turn everything into some big fag joke?

Pause. The others are mystified, including Charles, who rearranges himself on the floor.

JOE   I thought he was supposed to be fun.

TOM   James, what's wrong?

JAMES   Nothing . . . I shouldn't have come.

JOE   Maybe not.

TOM   Joe!

JOE   I know he's your friend, but he's been a real downer since he got here.

JAMES   I guess it was inevitable. Sorry to spoil the fun. Really, I . . . See ya.

TOM   No, James, wait.

MICHAEL   Let him go if he wants to.

TOM   Please, James, we're your friends. Talk to us.

JAMES   I'm telling you, *I'm* fine. I actually came here to share happy news . . . This isn't right; I'm just going to go.

BRAD Oh, for God's sake, stop being such a drama queen and spill it.

JAMES I'm getting married.

TOM To . . . ?

JAMES A woman. That sounds so . . . Susan. My friend. I brought her to your party that time. Then we had dinner . . .

TOM I remember. She's still in my address book.

MICHAEL She was nice.

JAMES Yes. She is.

Pause.

TOM Next question. *Why?*

BRAD Thank you.

TOM Are you straight now, is that it?

Brad scoffs at the idea.

CHARLES It happens.

BRAD No it doesn't.

JAMES No. I'm not straight.

JOE Does she know that?

JAMES Of course. She knows everything.

TOM Then why . . . ?

JAMES I can't do this anymore.

TOM "This?"

JAMES All of it. This "community," if anyone can call it that without laughing. It holds nothing for me anymore. It's not what I want. So I'm getting married.

CHARLES Now *that's* post-gay.

JOE Well, that's great, good luck to you. We're missing the go-go boys.

Joe goes to the window.

BRAD This is so weird. Guys usually get married *before* I sleep with them.

TOM I don't know how we're supposed to react to this.

JAMES It would be nice if you could be happy for me. But I guess that's too much to ask.

TOM James, you wrote a gay novel. It was published; you were crucified in the *Advocate*.

CHARLES Sounds like you're past the point of no return.

TOM Oh, wait. Is this because of the book?

JAMES What?

TOM Your book. Is this because you got bad reviews?

JAMES No, of course not.

MICHAEL They were pretty mean.

JAMES They were right. *Circuit Boy* was a fake, written from the outside. No. I don't belong, I never did. I was glad they pointed it out.

JOE (*Watching the parade*) There's the cast of *Curious George*. They're playing volleyball.

TOM Joe, we're having a serious conversation.

JOE I know. And I don't like where it's going.

CHARLES I'm with you.

MICHAEL   So it wasn't the reviews.

JAMES   My rejection by the Gay Establishment was a gift. It got me started, wondering. Why did I feel so shitty all the time? I mean, I'm a smart, reasonably attractive guy. What was going on? So I decided to investigate. I plunged into "the scene."

MICHAEL   Bad idea.

JAMES   I went out every night . . .

BRAD   I saw you at the White Party.

JAMES   You did? You didn't say hello.

BRAD   From a distance. You were dancing like a maniac.

JAMES   I was miserable.

TOM   Of course you were. Dancing with twinkies tweaked out of their minds. It's empty and depressing.

JAMES   And I wanted to be part of it so badly. I felt this . . . *want* that stemmed from someplace really deep, someplace I'm ashamed of. I'm still a competitive kid from the Ivy League. I only enjoy doing things I'm good at. And I'm not good at this.

TOM   So you're giving up.

JAMES   I'm saving myself.

CHARLES   Oh, God. I've seen this before. He's going to take out a pamphlet.

TOM   Saving yourself from what? Drugs and a bad dance mix?

BRAD   You don't like it, go online.

JAMES   I did; it was a disaster.

CHARLES   Well, then find a piano bar.

JAMES   I tried that, too. I sat in the Duplex for three weeks, drinking cosmos, trying to hide the fact I don't know the harmony part in "I Feel Pretty."

Joe gasps in shock.

JAMES (*cont.*)   I met a guy there. A cute landscape architect. We hit it off. I thought, Okay, this is good, I'm doing well. So I kissed him.

MICHAEL   And?

JAMES   He told me I should cut down on my carbs.

TOM   What a dickhead. I'm so sorry.

CHARLES (*Unmoved*)   Yes, yes, it's criminal. But, um, this was a really hot guy, right?

JAMES   You could say that.

CHARLES   Well, I'm sorry, but them's the rules. I don't mean to be unsympathetic, but you have to face facts; we all do. There's a hierarchy. The rules are clear and strictly enforced.

TOM   You can't go by one guy.

JAMES   I didn't. I met plenty of guys who were interested in me.

MICHAEL   And?

JAMES   They weren't my type. Fat. Effeminate. I don't like that.

JOE   Hello?

TOM   Do you hear yourself?

JAMES   Yes, of course I do. I'm as bad as the rest.

JOE   Men are pigs.

BRAD   Especially the ones who won't sleep with me.

JAMES   Anyway, everything finally made sense when I went to see my sister, Melissa.

TOM   I remember her from school.

BRAD   The skinny girl.

JAMES   She's anorexic.

BRAD   Oops.

Covering for his faux pas, Brad ducks behind the kitchen counter. He rises slowly for James's next speech.

JAMES   I came home from another pathetic night of cruising to hear this frantic message from my parents. "Melissa's in the hospital, we need you to come home." Of course, the irony did not escape me. I had always pictured the family gathered around *my* hospital bed, saying they love me, apologizing for not understanding. I missed out on that noble gay scenario.

BRAD   It's not too late.

JAMES   When I got there, Melissa was hooked up to an IV. She couldn't carry on a conversation, her brain was barely functioning—not enough nutrients in her system. She looked like something out of Bergen-Belsen. I just stood and stared at her. She had done that to herself. And all I could think was . . . how much I admired her discipline.

CHARLES   Jesus.

JOE   You've got problems.

JAMES I'm telling you the truth. That's what I thought. And that's when I understood. I was just like her. I couldn't stand to look at myself in the mirror. I knew the insecurity, the need to be something I wasn't. I just lacked the strength to do anything about it.

JOE You want my trainer's number? He's certified.

TOM Joe . . .

JAMES I knew if I didn't do something, I'd end up like Melissa, or dead. So I got out.

TOM And registered for stemware.

JAMES Susan is the best person I know. We love each other.

TOM She's all right with this?

JAMES We think it makes sense for both of us.

BRAD So . . . will you fuck her?

MICHAEL Oh, God.

CHARLES There's a pertinent question.

JAMES Not that it's any of your business, but we don't plan on it. If it happens later, that's fine, but we've decided not to focus on it.

BRAD That'll last.

JAMES I didn't think you would understand.

BRAD Hey, it's all about getting your needs met. Your sister ignored what her body was telling her. Look what happened.

JAMES Some needs are more important than others.

TOM Like your need to feel better than the rest of us.

56

JAMES I don't. I just don't feel worse. Not anymore.

JOE I'm glad to hear it. Good-bye.

TOM I can't believe this.

MICHAEL Why do you care so much?

TOM Because it's not natural.

CHARLES That may not be our most winning argument.

MICHAEL If he thinks he'll be happy, good for him.

JAMES Thank you.

MICHAEL Whatever.

TOM No. I'm sorry, there's more to it than that. You are a gay man. There are responsibilities.

JAMES Such as?

TOM To be . . . true to your orientation. To fight the fight.

JAMES Fight for what?

TOM For the right to be who we are. So we don't have to lie anymore.

JAMES I'm not lying to anyone.

TOM Yes you are. To yourself. Come on, James. You'll marry Susan, like some closet case from the fifties with a stash of muscle magazines in the attic, and you'll walk down Eighth Avenue bombarded by images of all the things you can't have.

JAMES I do that now. At least I'll have something else.

TOM So you're just going to throw in the towel. Leave the rest of us to carry on the struggle.

Charles starts to laugh.

TOM (*cont.*)   What?

CHARLES   I'm sorry. I don't mean to switch sides or anything, but what the hell are you talking about? To what struggle are you referring?

TOM   Ours. Against straight oppression.

CHARLES   Oh, that one. Funny, I didn't see you there.

TOM   What does that mean?

CHARLES   Have you ever been arrested? Any of you?

BRAD (*Singing*)   "We shall overcome . . ."

CHARLES   I'm just saying, we had a march, you have a parade. So it's a bit curious to hear you boys talking about "the struggle" when the bravest thing you ever did was sneak into the gay and lesbian student dance your junior year. You have no idea how lucky you are. You have no idea how much it fucked us up, living with all that hate. And shame. I hope you never do.

TOM   Yes, you're right, we've had it easy, too easy. But that's why we have a responsibility to honor the people who paved the way years and years ago . . .

CHARLES   God, I walked right into that one.

TOM   We have a duty to fight until we are truly recognized in the culture . . .

JAMES   Are you serious? We're already overexposed. The culture's learned everything from us. Cute boys rule the world. No one will read a book unless the author looks good in flat fronts and something ribbed. The war's over. We won.

CHARLES   Maybe in the arts. Maybe in New York, L.A., and San Francisco. But there are still kids being beaten up and left on fences out there.

JAMES   Yes, they suffer and take abuse until they escape to the Emerald City where they dance at the Morning Party with David Geffen. If they're lucky, they'll become porn stars.

JOE   Is this like the second half of a gay play? The part where it turns really dark and annoying and everyone wallows in self-hatred?

JAMES   A little self-hatred may not be such a bad thing.

CHARLES   Oh, yes. (*À la Boys in the Band*)   "If only we didn't *like* ourselves quite so much. If only we didn't *like* ourselves quite so very much."

Charles mimes slitting his wrists.

JAMES   Look out there. You tell me.

TOM   You can't judge us by the parade. We're not a part of that.

BRAD   We just watch from the window.

TOM   What's down there is not representative and you know it. There are all kinds of gay people. Bankers, lawyers, dentists . . .

MICHAEL   I didn't see you running to the window to look for dentists.

TOM   Why is everyone picking on me?

MICHAEL   We're not picking on you, sweetie.

CHARLES   Just don't try to argue with this guy. You can't win. He says, "Gay men are all narcissistic and shallow." It's too easy. He forgets those hunks became that way because they didn't want to be picked on anymore.

JAMES So it's an act of bravery, not vanity, to go to the gym six times a week?

CHARLES Absolutely. It's a defense mechanism. Like gay humor.

JAMES Oh, please.

CHARLES You don't appreciate gay humor?

JAMES Camp? It's just sophomoric sex jokes and quotes from straight movie stars at their most grotesque.

BRAD Not true! Sometimes we put on women's clothing.

CHARLES Oh, I've seen that. That's very funny.

TOM You hear that witty banter?

JAMES My head is spinning.

CHARLES Well, you should have heard the laughs we were getting before you came in.

JAMES Okay. So we're the shining examples of "the life." You think those frightened gay kids out there should want to grow up to be like us?

When the others don't answer, Joe bursts out:

JOE Yes! Of course they should! My God, what is wrong with all of you? You just let him go on . . .

TOM Joe, it's all right.

JOE No, it's not. I was one of those kids. And I don't know what I would have done if I didn't find my way here.

BRAD New York?

60

JOE No. Here. To a room full of gay men. A room full of people who get my jokes. Who get *me*. I like being a part of this. I like eating in restaurants and watching the straight people try to figure out why we're having so much fun. I wouldn't give it up for anything. Maybe the rest of you take it for granted but I don't. Should anyone be like us? If they're lucky.

CHARLES From the mouths of babes.

JOE Don't patronize me.

CHARLES I'm not, I swear. It took me a lot longer to get where you are. To say, "I want this, I'd choose this." Good for you.

JOE Thank you. (*Proud, walking to the window.*) Now I want to look at cute boys.

BRAD Make room.

JAMES Well, that's inspiring. I guess I'm the only one here who even knows what I'm talking about.

TOM Apparently you are.

MICHAEL No. You're not.

TOM What?

MICHAEL I understand, James. I do.

TOM You'd rather be straight?

MICHAEL I don't know. I've thought about it. Oh, come on, we all have at one time or another.

TOM Thanks for telling me.

MICHAEL I'm just saying, there are times . . . There are times when I wonder what it means. Gay. Me, gay. Is it about

61

who I sleep with? My CD collection, what? I'll be in the middle of something, at the movies, reading the paper, and I stop. Is this it? This life, living in the city with my boyfriend. Summer weekends on Fire Island. AIDS benefits with Chita Rivera. Is this it? Was this what I was meant for?

CHARLES That's not a gay thing, that's regret. Everybody has it.

MICHAEL Maybe. But why does it all feel so foreign sometimes? I don't feel fabulous. Aren't we supposed to feel fabulous?

TOM We've been together seven years and now you tell me you wish you were straight?

MICHAEL That's not what I said.

JAMES He's just being honest.

TOM Oh, shut up, James. So, you're saying if you could, you'd be straight.

MICHAEL I don't know. Maybe.

TOM Oh, God.

JOE It's a ridiculous question.

BRAD (*Waving to James*) Apparently not.

TOM I don't know how to deal with this.

MICHAEL Don't get so upset. It's not like I can. And it's not like I'm unhappy with you.

TOM You're not?

MICHAEL Not very.

TOM What?!

MICHAEL   I'm kidding. No, I'm not unhappy.

TOM   This is a nightmare.

BRAD   Tom, take it easy. It's James, this is what he does.

JAMES   What is?

BRAD   You tear down what you can't have. You're a walking sour grape; you always were. When we went out, all you did was talk about Tom. How hypocritical he was, how self-involved.

TOM   You did?

MICHAEL   Well, this is interesting.

BRAD   Same as now. You were all self-righteous and pissy because you'd been dumped on your ass and couldn't take it.

JAMES   That's the first thing anyone's said that I agree with. It's true. I'm sorry, Tom. I said terrible things.

TOM   That's okay.

JAMES   It's just . . . I loved you. You probably don't even remember.

TOM   Of course I do. It was a nice time.

JAMES   You loved me, too. I felt it.

TOM   (*Uncomfortable*)   Sure, I guess.

JAMES   You were my first, I mean, the first that mattered.

TOM   That was a long time ago.

JAMES   I still remember what it felt like. When it was all so new.

TOM   All right, James, that's enough.

MICHAEL No, let him finish.

JAMES It felt like we were the only ones in the world. Sneaking around campus. Kissing in the library, cryptic phone calls in front of the roommates. Like we invented romance.

MICHAEL Sounds like the real thing.

TOM We didn't know any better.

JAMES And everything we did, everything we said to each other, it was all in code. Our own secret language. God, I pity the kids now, with their gay support groups in the first grade.

CHARLES They still have romance.

JAMES But the code made it interesting. The code made it special. I was happy then, before I had to declare anything. I think about those days a lot. And you know what's funny, I can't remember what your abs looked like. I don't think I noticed.

BRAD You were twenty. You had them anyway.

CHARLES I'll bet the kids notice now.

JAMES Whose fault is that?

JOE So we care about how we look—why is that so terrible? You want to walk around looking like the average straight person, go ahead. The average gay man could have straight women hanging all over him.

BRAD The average gay man *does* have straight women hanging all over him.

TOM And all we have to do is pick one desperate enough to marry us.

JAMES   Susan's not desperate and neither am I. I'm just turning it off. All of it. The sleazy magazines, the strippers on cable access, the parades. I'm done.

TOM   Well, so are we. Those things have nothing to do with being gay and you know it. Look at Michael and me.

MICHAEL   Tom, please don't . . .

TOM   We are completely removed from the gay scene.

JAMES   You live on *Christopher Street!*

TOM   We're moving to Nyack!

JAMES   And you think *I'm* giving up? If things are so peachy, why are you running away?

TOM   We're not running. We are proving that we can live anywhere. Because we're secure in who we are. We don't read the bar rags and we don't watch the naked guys on cable access . . .

MICHAEL   At least not together.

TOM   Let me tell you something. You think you can't have a fulfilling, stable, loving life as a gay couple? You think you'll never feel the way we did in college? Well, that is simply not true. Anyone in this room can have what Michael and I have if he really wants it. You don't believe it's possible? Just look at us.

Brad turns on the juicer. The noise rattles everyone.

TOM (*cont.*)   Turn that off! Damn it, Brad! Turn it off!

Brad pretends that he can't hear until Tom turns the juicer off.

TOM (*cont.*)   Very funny.

MICHAEL   Why did you do that?

TOM   He's just being a smart-ass.

MICHAEL   I want to hear it from him. Brad?

BRAD   I just thought Tom was getting a little carried away.

JAMES   Is there something I'm missing?

JOE   Turning on the juicer means someone is lying. It's a cheap theatrical device we set up before your entrance.

MICHAEL   What do you know, Brad?

TOM   Nothing. This is silly.

MICHAEL   Brad?

BRAD   Oh, come on, it's not like it's some big secret.

TOM   Brad, don't, really . . .

BRAD   Tom, you told me about your "arrangement." It's fine. If you want to see other people and get laid when you're away on business, whatever, that's between the two of you. But don't stand there and pretend to be Mr. and Mrs. James fucking Brolin.

MICHAEL   Oh, my God.

BRAD   (*Disingenuous*)   Oops.

MICHAEL   You've been fucking around? And everybody knows it?

TOM   I have not been "fucking around." I've . . . there have been . . . a few times . . . Oh, come on, Michael, we talked about this.

JOE   I'm checking my mail.

Joe goes to the computer to check his e-mail.

TOM   We had this conversation; you know we did. We agreed, after all this time, if either of us were in a situation, we said it was okay . . .

MICHAEL   I seem to remember some vague, baffling talk that ended in you making a joke and me saying "whatever." Was that the one?

TOM   Yes.

MICHAEL   Well, clearly your friends have a much better understanding of our "arrangement" than I do. I must have lost the talking points.

TOM   You're being totally unfair.

MICHAEL   I am?

Michael heads for the bedroom but Tom blocks his way.

TOM   All right, you want to know about them? Let's see, last March, in Chicago . . .

MICHAEL   Stop, I don't want to hear it! Not now!

TOM   I will not let myself be made out to be the bad guy here, like I'm the only guy who's ever . . . It doesn't mean anything real. Men are geared to look around; we can't help it.

CHARLES   It's a fact of evolution.

TOM   All men fool around; they always did.

JAMES   My father didn't.

CHARLES   Mine didn't.

Finished with the computer, Joe goes to the kitchen.

JOE Mine didn't.

BRAD Mine did.

TOM You see?

BRAD But he doesn't count.

TOM Why not?

BRAD He was gay.

CHARLES Really?

BRAD You'd think it would be a cool thing, to find out you had a gay dad. It wasn't. He was a mess.

TOM Of course. Because of the lying, the secrecy. God, everyone gets so crazy over sex. But—but—but we're more honest about it than straight people. Right? We recognize the difference between love and sex.

BRAD Get your needs met.

TOM Exactly. Sex is not the cornerstone of a loving relationship.

JAMES I couldn't have said it better myself.

TOM Will you *shut up!*

MICHAEL You don't know when to stop, do you? You can spout this garbled free love crap all night, but it's too late, Tom.

TOM We talked about it.

MICHAEL No, you did. I don't know why I'm surprised. You've always been a flirt. You can't say hello to any of your cute friends without a big wet kiss on the lips.

JOE That is true.

BRAD   I felt tongue.

TOM   You did not!

CHARLES   You never kiss me.

TOM   Here, you want a kiss?

CHARLES   No, no, them's the rules.

MICHAEL   You see? You hug and kiss and run around trying to make everybody love you. I should have known it didn't end there.

TOM   Michael . . .

MICHAEL   (*Walking to the door*)   I'm going out for a while. Good luck, James. Let me know if she has a sister.

Another roar from the juicer stops Michael in his tracks. This time Joe flipped the switch.

TOM   What now?

JOE   I'm sorry, Michael, but Tom has been a good friend for a long time.

MICHAEL   So?

JOE   So you can't walk out of here acting all wounded like you've never even thought about other guys.

MICHAEL   How would you know?

JOE   We had cybersex.

MICHAEL   That's a lie!

TOM   Oh, God.

JOE   Sorry, Tom. I didn't know it was Michael for sure until I just saw your other screen name, "CUTEMIKE4." I thought it was you when you described yourself, although "swimmer build" is a reach.

MICHAEL   Why didn't you tell me who you were?

JOE   Online? Actually, it made the whole thing kind of kinky.

BRAD (*Writing it down*)   "CUTEMIKE4." Was he any good?

TOM   Brad!

MICHAEL   Doing stuff online is different than . . .

JOE   We talked about hooking up.

MICHAEL   But we didn't! We never did, did we?

JOE   No.

MICHAEL   You see? It's not the same! And you go out of town, or to the opera with Charles, and I'm left here alone . . .

TOM   Sweetie, it's okay. I mean, not with Joe, but I understand. We've been together a long time and there's all this stuff out there that's so goddamn available. You can't be expected to . . .

MICHAEL (*Walking slowly to the bedroom*)   Yes I can. Shit, this is so . . . I want to lie down.

Michael exits to the bedroom and closes the door. Tom tries to follow, but the door is locked.

TOM   Honey? Michael, please. (*He turns to the others.*)   I guess I fucked up.

JOE   You both did.

CHARLES   It happens. More often than not.

TOM But I . . . I did stupid things. He stopped online.

BRAD Nobody stops online.

TOM What?

BRAD Come on. Nobody stops at flirting online. It doesn't happen.

TOM Well, you're the expert.

BRAD Excuse me?

TOM I don't want to talk about it with you, all right? Michael didn't do anything wrong.

BRAD Suit yourself.

TOM Damn it, Brad. Why did you start that? What possessed you?

BRAD I didn't know it was such a secret.

TOM Bullshit.

BRAD All right. Maybe I was tired of you preaching the gospel of the perfect gay couple. Tom and Michael have it all. Well, I'm really happy for you. But that's you. We don't all meet a nice guy at twenty-five and settle down for a lifetime of almost monogamy. We may not want to. Some of us have other ways of going through life and we don't want to feel like we're failures. Or sick.

TOM No. I'm sorry.

BRAD You just get so smug.

TOM I'm sorry.

CHARLES Will he be okay?

TOM   Yeah, sure. We'll pull through. We always do, right? (*Beat.*)   It's funny, you don't know when it happens, but then one day it hits you, you're *fused*. Anything else is . . . unimaginable.

JOE   It'll work out. I'm sure it will.

TOM   Thanks.

JAMES   I didn't mean for this to happen.

TOM   If you say so.

JAMES   I just came to tell you my plans. It was your other friends who tried to sabotage your relationship. But this has never been a community that supports long-term couples . . .

CHARLES   You know, I just remembered another thing that always bothers me about gay plays. There's always one nasty character who causes trouble and makes everybody feel like shit. And I always wonder, who invited him? Why are they friends with this asshole and why don't they tell him to leave?

They all turn to James.

JAMES   I'm leaving.

JOE   So soon?

JAMES   I'll send you a postcard from our honeymoon.

JOE   Where are you going?

JAMES   South Beach.

BRAD   Good choice.

JAMES   We had a coupon!

TOM   You're wrong, James. You won't walk out of here as some conquering hero of the "gay menace." Because I know you, James. I remember you. And I won't let you say that my life has been a waste of time . . .

JAMES I never said that.

TOM We've worked too hard; we've made a commitment. You're unhappy? Well, maybe you're just an unhappy person. You ever think of that? Maybe it's not "society's fault." Maybe you're just fucked up, James. You don't need a wife, you need a therapist, because you'll be just as miserable on the other side!

JAMES We'll see.

TOM Don't do this. You'll ruin your life!

JAMES Say good-bye to Michael for me.

As James exits, Tom calls out:

TOM This can't happen! It won't!

James is gone. Pause.

JOE I guess I'll go back down.

BRAD I'll come with.

CHARLES Me too.

JOE Okay.

Charles peeks out the door to make sure James is gone. Joe kisses Tom on the shoulder; then he and Charles exit. Brad stops at the door.

BRAD Tom, you okay? Look, I'm sorry about . . .

TOM Whatever.

BRAD You and Michael can never break up. It would be like Lucy and Desi all over again. People crying in the streets.

Brad pretends to cry on Tom's shoulder. Tom smiles, the tension between them diminished. Brad exits. Tom goes to the bedroom door. It's still locked.

TOM   Michael? Please, talk to me. I'm sorry, I shouldn't have called him. But we can't let him get to us, you know? He's the one with the problem, not us. What do I have to do?

Blackout.

SCENE FOUR

Charles, Brad, and Joe are back, talking to Tom. Michael is still in the bedroom with the door closed. Charles thumbs through the CD collection.

BRAD   An intervention?

TOM   Something like that.

JOE   This is so exciting! Like we're fighting the Moonies.

CHARLES   This is why we were summoned back here? You know, they charge me when you call my cell phone . . .

BRAD   You actually spoke to her?

TOM   Her number was still in my book. I asked her to come over.

BRAD   You're a bit obsessed with this, aren't you?

TOM   This is important for all of us. Why do you think James came over here today?

JOE   You called him.

BRAD   And he's still in love with you.

TOM   No, please. He didn't have to come. He didn't have to tell us. No, he shows up on Gay Pride to say he's getting married because he wants us to stop him from making a horrible mistake.

BRAD   I don't know.

TOM   This is a defining moment.

CHARLES   (*Holding up a CD*)   You know, they remastered this *Tristan*.

TOM   Can we stay focused here?

BRAD   He really got under your skin.

TOM   No, because he's wrong. Making us all sound like sex-obsessed fourteen-year-olds. A race of Bill Clintons, ready to chuck everything for a blowjob.

BRAD   I, for one, have no problem accepting my sex drive.

JOE   "Get your needs met!"

BRAD   And neither do my disciples. I like to look, I can't help it. My day is a constant calculation of cute/not-cute, cute/not-cute, like a bleary-eyed judge at an endless beauty pageant. That is how I live my life. Now, I could get all upset and slit my wrists or marry some fag hag, but I just don't feel the need. I enjoy it.

CHARLES   (*Faint enthusiasm*)   Here here.

JOE   I'm going back to the window.

TOM   Doesn't it make you feel empty?

BRAD   Not particularly.

TOM   Frustrated?

CHARLES Tired?

BRAD It used to. But then I set different goals. I don't have to sleep with every guy I see. I just want to sleep with one of every representative type.

CHARLES How's it going?

BRAD Find me a gay albino and I'm done.

Michael comes out of the bedroom. He flips on the kitchen lights and returns a glass to the sink.

TOM Hey.

MICHAEL Is she coming?

TOM You heard. I think so.

MICHAEL I'll say hi, and make sure you don't say anything stupid.

Michael sits. Charles and Brad join Joe at the window.

JOE God, the parade is still going. Look at it down there, it's like a giant gay ant farm.

CHARLES Leni Riefenstahl meets Calvin Klein. Completely fascinating and utterly uninteresting.

BRAD I feel like last year there were more tattoos.

The intercom buzzes. Tom presses the buzzer to open the door without asking who it is.

TOM That's her.

JOE This is so exciting! What does she look like? Is she fat? I picture her fat with dirty hair.

MICHAEL I think she's pretty.

CHARLES Well, then something else is wrong with her.

TOM She's just deluded. We have to show her that James is wrong. That we're not all shallow and boy crazy.

The doorbell rings. Tom opens it to reveal SCOTT, *twenty-six, a buff and beautiful young man wearing no shirt. He is breathtaking.*

SCOTT Hey. (*Beat.*) Is this a bad time?

BRAD, JOE, & CHARLES *No!*

SCOTT Oh, good. Hey, Tommy.

He gives Tom a kiss on the lips. Tom squirms.

TOM Everybody, this is Scott. Brad, Charles, Joe . . .

JOE (*Tongue-tied*) I saw you, before, down at the grocery store, talking to Tom, before.

SCOTT Cool.

TOM And this is Michael, my boyfriend Michael.

SCOTT Oh, that's right, I think you said you were seeing someone.

TOM We've been together seven years.

SCOTT That's great.

TOM The best.

SCOTT (*To Michael*) Have we met before? You look familiar.

MICHAEL No, Tom's never introduced us.

SCOTT My mistake. So, Tom, I hate to intrude on your party but I was wondering if I could use your bathroom.

TOM Oh . . .

SCOTT I drank like a whole bottle of Gatorade and I really can't face one of those "Here's Johnny's" down there. They're so disgusting and the line is forever . . .

BRAD (*Flirting, getting closer*) I hate that.

SCOTT I remembered you said I should stop by . . .

TOM Of course, go ahead.

SCOTT Cool. I'll be quick—I told my friends to wait for me.

Scott heads for the bathroom even before Tom says . . .

TOM It's right through there.

SCOTT Yeah, right. Thanks, guy.

Scott exits to the bathroom.

BRAD Did you see the way he looked at me? He wants me and he doesn't care who knows it.

TOM I didn't think he'd come.

MICHAEL Clearly, *Tommy.*

JOE "I saw you. Before." Shit, I'm such an idiot.

CHARLES He had to come. It was inevitable.

TOM It was?

CHARLES Of course. The unexpected arrival of the shirtless hunk. You can't have a gay play without one.

MICHAEL Isn't he supposed to be ethnic?

CHARLES This guy will do.

BRAD Anyone he wants.

JOE It does make sense. Who else would we put on the poster?

CHARLES The hunk always comes in, raises the heat, says a few stupid lines, and exits.

BRAD And comes home with me. (*To God or the playwright.*) Just a suggestion.

TOM How can you go on like this after everything that's happened today?

BRAD If we don't, the terrorists win!

The toilet flushes.

TOM Be nice.

Scott comes out of the bedroom.

SCOTT Wow, thanks. I had to pee like a racehorse.

BRAD I knew it!

SCOTT (*Looking out the window*) So you guys have been watching the parade from here? That's great.

JOE (*Tongue tied again*) You can see everything. I mean, not everything, but you can see . . . a lot.

BRAD I was down there for a while but I got so tired of being hit on.

SCOTT Yeah. God, look at 'em all, checking each other out. Michelangelo's David couldn't get a phone number down there. They'd tell him to work on his delts.

Brad, Joe, and Charles laugh a bit too heartily at the joke.

JOE That's really funny . . . really.

SCOTT Man, the gay world is brutal.

CHARLES Excuse me? How can you say that?

SCOTT It's the truth.

JOE Yeah, but you're so incredible. I mean, physically . . .

SCOTT Thanks, that's sweet of you to say. But you know how it goes. There's always somebody coming round the corner a few years younger with a few more inches. (*Beat.*) I should get going, my friends are . . .

BRAD, JOE, & CHARLES No!

BRAD What's the rush? Do you want something to drink?

SCOTT Actually, some water would be great. I need to rehydrate.

BRAD (*Snapping for service*) Tom, could you?

Tom glares at Brad and gets a bottle of water for Scott. Scott sees the copy of Circuit Boy *and picks it up.*

SCOTT Oh, God, *Circuit Boy.*

CHARLES Did you read it?

SCOTT Yeah. I read it in my book group. I didn't like it. If I remember correctly, no one did.

TOM The author's an old friend.

SCOTT (*Putting the book back down*) Oh, whoops. Sorry.

TOM (*Handing Scott the water*) That's okay. We didn't like it either.

SCOTT Thanks. Yeah, I don't know. He has some talent, it was well structured, but that's not enough anymore, you know? I mean, how many tortured coming-out stories or disillusioned-by-sex-in-the-city books can we take? At this point, I really can't read another gay novel. Maybe that makes me a bad homo but I just don't respond automatically like I used to. I don't like being taken for granted.

Scott drinks the water as the group watches in awe.

JOE So do you take steroids?

TOM Joe!

JOE What? We were talking about it before and I was wondering . . .

SCOTT Well, let me just say, I don't think they're a good idea for everyone. But my roommate's a trainer with a nutrition degree, so if I was going to do them, I'd do them the right way.

BRAD "Roommate." Is that a euphemism?

SCOTT No, just a roommate.

BRAD Good to know.

SCOTT I've sort of given up looking for a boyfriend.

JOE Why's that?

SCOTT It's just so hard to find a gay man who isn't fucked up. I guess you can't really blame them.

CHARLES Many people do.

SCOTT I've been burned too many times, meeting guys at bars or on the computer—which is really stupid; you never know what kind of creep is typing on the other end.

TOM (*Looking at Joe*) Yeah, we know.

SCOTT But hey, the way I see it, it's all about getting your needs met, right?

BRAD (*To the heavens*) Thank you.

SCOTT Once, I went to meet this guy on the Upper West Side and . . . no, forget it, stupid story.

BRAD I doubt that.

JOE Tell us.

CHARLES I want to hear.

SCOTT Well, he greets me at the door in a kimono. He looks nothing like he said he did—he's older and I think he was wearing a wig—but hey, I was looking for some kind of human encounter. I figured, I'll go in, I'll talk to him, then make a graceful exit.

BRAD That's really nice of you.

SCOTT Wait. So we go in, I sit down, and he opens his kimono. And there, on his chest, were two fully developed female breasts. And he looks at me with this expression of such pride, like "Boy, did *you* hit the jackpot!"

CHARLES Maybe some guys like that.

TOM No guys like that.

SCOTT You'd think he might have mentioned it before I got on the subway. Like, "Did you enjoy *The Crying Game?*"

JOE What did you do?

SCOTT I stared at him and I thought to myself, How did I get here? What in my life brought me to . . . this? And then I got out of there so fast, I think I broke his door. It was so sad. He looked at me like he had this gift and I could be the one to accept it. I was the answer to his prayers. I don't want that responsibility. Not with anyone.

The intercom buzzes. Tom presses the button to let Susan in.

TOM That's her, that's Susan.

SCOTT Who's Susan?

82

JOE James, the guy who wrote *Circuit Boy,* is getting married. To a woman, Susan.

SCOTT No shit. So he's going straight?

CHARLES Something like that.

SCOTT Well, my book group will be happy. Hey, if it brings him some peace, more power to him. The way I see it, the old rules didn't make much sense, and the new ones aren't any better. No one knows how we're supposed to be anymore. I think people just have to make it up as they go along. As long as they tell each other the truth.

CHARLES You're a very smart guy.

SCOTT I get that a lot. I just wish people didn't sound so surprised when they say it.

The doorbell rings. Tom opens the door for SUSAN, *thirty-three. She's nice-looking, with a warm, intelligent smile.*

TOM Hi, thanks for coming. I'm Tom.

SUSAN Of course you are, I remember. How are you? How are things at the firm?

TOM Fine.

SUSAN Oh, and there's Michael. God, you guys look great.

MICHAEL Thanks. So do you.

SUSAN Oh, please. This is my *schlumpy* Sunday look. But I figured, no one's looking at me today.

TOM This is Charles, Brad, Joe, and this is Scott.

SUSAN My, my. I thought I saw all the gay men in the world downstairs. And now here you all are.

SCOTT   I was just leaving.

SUSAN   I hope it's not because of me.

SCOTT   No, I have friends waiting. Thanks, Tommy.

TOM   Don't mention it.

SCOTT   See you guys.

BRAD   You know, Scott, I'd love to hear more about your book club. I've always wanted to join one.

SCOTT   Well, actually, we sort of have too many people right now.

BRAD   Oh, come on. Even Oprah could always pull up another chair. Why don't you give me your number . . . ?

SCOTT   Um, that's okay, I'll get yours from Tom sometime.

BRAD   Excellent. And try to ditch your friends so you can come back up here. I bet we're more fun.

SCOTT   Yeah, I'll try. Take care. Nice meeting you all. (*To Susan.*)   And good luck to you. Hang in there. Bye.

Scott exits.

SUSAN   Well, he seemed nice. Oh, Michael, I brought you something. I remember when we had dinner, I told you about this series of children's books we represent, *Chrissy the Caterpillar.* I kept meaning to send them to you. They never really caught on but I think your kids will love them.

She gives three books to Michael.

MICHAEL   Thank you, I remember. That's really sweet.

JOE   You're in publishing?

SUSAN   A small literary agency.

TOM   That's how you met James.

SUSAN   Right. We sold *Circuit Boy*. Well, my boss did. James and I had this intriguing phone relationship for months. And then one night my boss had a party and we got paired up as partners for a game of celebrity.

CHARLES   What's that?

MICHAEL   You don't know celebrity?

JOE   Oh, it's this amazing game where everyone writes down ten names of famous people—actors, presidents, alive or dead, doesn't matter. Then when it's your turn, you pick the names out of a hat and you have to get your partner to say as many of them as you can in a minute. Like, "She's a singer married to Steve Lawrence."

TOM, MICHAEL, BRAD & SUSAN (*Involuntarily*)   Eydie Gorme!

JOE   You see?

CHARLES   That sounds great. I want to play.

TOM   No, you'll just throw in opera singers that no one can pronounce.

MICHAEL   People get pissed off when you're too obscure.

CHARLES   Everyone's heard of Tiziana Fabbricini.

TOM   No they haven't.

CHARLES   Well, it's time they did.

JOE   Maybe we *should* have a game. It's required for the play, isn't it? Secrets are revealed and it ends badly . . .

SUSAN   What is he talking about?

MICHAEL All day, they've been saying how this could be a gay play—us in this apartment, with the parade outside.

SUSAN Oh, I see. But if this were a gay play, I wouldn't be here, would I?

TOM No, probably not.

SUSAN I'd be doing costumes.

BRAD I like this chick.

SUSAN (*Pleased*) Thank you. "Chick."

TOM Anyway, so you're playing celebrity . . .

SUSAN Oh, right. And James and I just clicked. We had both put in Roxie Roker.

CHARLES Who?

EVERYBODY ELSE Mrs. Willis on *The Jeffersons.*

CHARLES Oh, that's not obscure . . .

SUSAN I mean, what are the odds, right? We stayed up that whole night talking. And now . . . here we are.

TOM Yeah. That's what we wanted to know.

SUSAN Here it comes. You think I'm insane, don't you? Go ahead, give it your best shot.

TOM You have to admit, this whole idea of the two of you . . .

SUSAN Pretty freaky, huh? My mother tells people I'm marrying a foreigner so he can get his green card. Which I suspect is how you see it, too.

JOE Are you a lesbian?

MICHAEL Joe!

JOE What? It's a fair question.

SUSAN No, alas, I am not.

JOE Are you a fag hag?

TOM & MICHAEL Joe!

JOE What?

SUSAN God, I hate that term. It's so demeaning.

MICHAEL I agree.

SUSAN It conjures this image of a woman hanging around a bunch of gay men bitching at each other, praying they'll ask her to dance before she goes home to feed her cats.

BRAD How many cats do you have?

SUSAN *One.* Okay, so I like gay men. I always have, ever since I was a teenager. I was one of those sensitive adolescent girls interested in horseback riding and homosexuals. You know the type.

JOE I was friends with a girl like that in drama club.

BRAD We all were.

SUSAN Yes, we're a proud stereotype. I guess the idea of a guy who wasn't determined to snap my bra strap really appealed to me. A boy who was like me, you know, who felt different. Who had some aesthetic sense. What can I say? I read *The Front Runner.*

CHARLES That'll do it.

SUSAN Then all of *Tales of the City,* David Leavitt, the *Buddies* trilogy . . . I somehow had an affinity for this stuff; I totally got it. So I was ready when all my friends came out in college. A lot of them told me first. I'm still proud of that.

MICHAEL   You should be.

SUSAN   Yeah. All the time I spent taking care of my boys. They were so dear to me.

CHARLES   Past tense. What happened?

SUSAN   Oh, I don't know. They joined "the scene" or whatever you call what's going on out the window. And I wasn't willing to go there with them.

CHARLES   Why not?

SUSAN   I started reading those books because I wanted to know about these people who had feelings and interests beyond those of the average fourteen-year-old. But then, when we graduated from college, all my gay male friends turned into the girls in my seventh-grade homeroom. "Ooh, did you see that guy? Ooh, do you think he's cute? Ooh, let's do facials."

Brad rises and moves away from Susan.

SUSAN (*cont.*)   I went through so much with them, all that drama, and then they buried what made them so special to me in the first place. What was in their hearts. So, to be honest, I pulled away. I went a long time keeping my distance from gay guys. Unless I went to the theater or the ballet or something.

At that, Joe moves away.

TOM   Until James.

SUSAN   Until James. Yeah, James was different. He'd been through the ringer. He needed someone safe he could open up to. I told him early on, I said, "I'm not going to be your fag hag, James. I'm not going to comfort you when that

88

bartender hasn't called in three days and then not mind when you don't call me for a month because he did."

CHARLES   You put conditions on a friendship?

SUSAN   Yes, I know, that was unfair, but I promised the same thing. I don't go on and on about how many bridesmaid dresses I have hanging in my closet or how loudly my biological clock is ticking. We have rules. We're determined to bring out only the best in each other.

TOM   You think playing house will "bring out the best" in him?

SUSAN   That's for James to decide, isn't it?

TOM   What about you? I mean, you're a pretty girl.

SUSAN   Gee, thanks ever so.

TOM   You can do better.

JOE   Have you tried dating?

SUSAN   Of course, yeah, whatever. But you know, *straight men.*

JOE   You poor thing.

SUSAN   They're fine, but, I don't know. Maybe I haven't met the right one or I'm too picky or it has something to do with my alcoholic mother—my therapist won't just come out and tell me what it is. But I always found myself wondering, Is the sex/marriage/baby component worth this? This guy, channel surfing in sweat socks, calling me "babe."

CHARLES   Sounds good to me.

MICHAEL   It wasn't for you.

SUSAN No, alas. And it was bringing me down. I can't tell you how many great women I know, cool "chicks," who are alone. And I know so few who are in a great marriage.

TOM So you decided to settle.

SUSAN I never really decided anything. It just evolved. We evolved.

TOM But you admit, this is a compromise.

SUSAN Show me a relationship that isn't. I'm willing to accept something less than perfection. Maybe you guys should try it sometime. What was his name? Scott?

BRAD Hey, don't knock the man I love. He's coming back for me.

SUSAN I hope you're very happy together. Whatever turns you on.

CHARLES "Get your needs met."

SUSAN Right. I finally know what I need.

BRAD And it's not sex.

SUSAN Shocking, isn't it?

TOM You know what will happen. The two of you will end up as nothing but glorified roommates.

SUSAN Sounds good to me. Isn't that what all couples become in the end, if they're lucky? It's having someone to live with. I always liked that phrase. To "live *with*" somebody, to share the burden. How long have you two been together?

MICHAEL Seven years.

SUSAN That's great.

TOM Thanks.

CHARLES Okay, this all sounds lovely and you seem like a very nice person. But, I'm sorry, he is a gay man. As Julie Andrews would say, "a homo-sex-sual." Do you honestly believe he'll be able to suppress that forever?

SUSAN No, of course not. But he wasn't able to pull the gay thing off.

TOM You don't pull it off, it's who you are!

SUSAN It's not that simple for James. You guys are happy in the life. He wasn't. He felt oppressed. Maybe someday he won't and he'll go out there and do what he has to, or I will, and we'll take it from there. Look, I know this is really strange and that you're threatened by it . . .

TOM (AND THE OTHERS AD-LIB) We are not threatened . . .

SUSAN Oh, of course you are. Otherwise you wouldn't have called me to "shake me down" or whatever it is you think you're doing. I understand. If it wasn't me, I'd probably get all outraged and call James and me terrible names—cowards, losers. But that night, when he pulled out the ring, I just . . .

CHARLES Ring?

She displays the ring on her finger. The guys admire it with an audible sigh.

SUSAN He put it on my finger and it felt right, and good. It was something real. So I said yes.

CHARLES It's beautiful. High quality.

SUSAN He went to five different places. This wasn't spur of the moment. It was the next step. The way I see it, we're like pioneers, heading out into unknown terrain.

JOE Homesteaders.

CHARLES Explorers.

BRAD Mormons.

SUSAN Something like that. We'll see what happens.

MICHAEL He's lucky to have you.

SUSAN Thank you. That means a lot. I hope we can all . . .

The intercom buzzes.

BRAD He came back! I knew it. How's my hair?

Tom goes to the intercom.

MICHAEL Check who it is this time.

TOM (*Into the intercom*) Hello?

JAMES (*On intercom*) It's James. Let me up.

TOM Oh, shit. What should I do?

JOE Stall him.

CHARLES Tell him you'll come down . . .

SUSAN He knows I'm here.

TOM What?

More buzzing.

SUSAN I left him a message.

Tom presses the button.

TOM Why did you do that? I asked you not to.

SUSAN What kind of marriage would this be if we started out keeping secrets from each other? I had to tell him where I was.

TOM Thanks a lot.

SUSAN He should know how much you care about him. He thought he didn't have any friends.

James pounds on the door. Tom opens it for him. James goes to Susan.

JAMES Are you all right?

SUSAN I'm fine. We were having a nice chat.

JAMES They tried to stop you, didn't they?

SUSAN It's all right, sweetie. They didn't really . . .

TOM We were worried about you.

JAMES Bullshit! You were worried about yourselves!

SUSAN James, don't.

JAMES You all have some fucking nerve. Saving me from her? Please. She saved me from you! Look at yourselves. "The girls who just watch." A bunch of hypocrites. Critics, thinking you're better than anybody. At least those guys out there on the street are part of something. At the center of something. They're authentic. You all are nothing!

Beat. James turns to Susan, his anger spent, embarrassed. He holds her.

JAMES (*cont.*) Sue? I'm sorry. I'm so sorry. I didn't mean to . . . Let's go home. Please? Let's go home.

SUSAN Yeah. Let's go home.

James exits. Susan follows but stops in the doorway.

SUSAN (*cont.*) It'll be okay. Don't worry. You'll see him again.

93

TOM I'm sure of it.

Susan exits. Pause.

MICHAEL Well, thanks for stopping by.

Michael returns to his original place by the window.

JOE Are we just going to take that?

CHARLES What do you want us to do?

JOE I don't know . . . Let's march!

BRAD What?

JOE Yeah! Fuck him! Let's show him. Let's show everybody! "We're here, we're queer, we're average and insecure . . ."

BRAD And horny.

JOE ". . . and horny, and confused, get used to it!" Come on, what do you say? We'll lock arms, the five of us, and march. We'll feel proud, really proud.

CHARLES Yes! Why not? Let's do it!

BRAD I'm in.

JOE This'll be great . . .

MICHAEL (*Looking out the window*) It's over.

JOE What?

MICHAEL The parade. It's over. Everybody's just milling around. Cruising.

JOE Well . . . next year. Right?

BRAD Yeah.

CHARLES It's a date.

JOE In the meantime, let's dance. I feel like dancing. Don't gay plays always end with a dance?

CHARLES Usually.

JOE Well? There's that big dance at the pier. Brad? Are you still waiting for Scott to come back?

BRAD I never wait for anyone.

JOE Then do you want to go dancing with me?

BRAD I'm dying to go dancing with you.

CHARLES That sounds great!

JOE Oh . . . yeah, we could go as a group.

CHARLES Oh, no. You guys have fun.

JOE You sure?

CHARLES Yeah, I have stuff to do.

JOE Okay. This'll be so fun.

BRAD Now, I warn you, I can get a little *handsy*.

JOE Uh-oh. Tom, is there anything else I should know about him?

TOM (*Thinks, then*) The usual. Proceed with caution.

BRAD Bye, guys. Call me next weekend. We'll go to the Quad and see another gay movie.

TOM Sounds good.

BRAD Remember what I said. Lucy and Desi.

JOE Come on!

BRAD Cute/not-cute . . . (*Pointing at Joe.*) Cute!

Joe laughs and Brad follows him out. Beat. Tom turns to Michael. Michael glances at Charles.

CHARLES   Well, I guess I'll go, too. I'm starving. You know, next time you guys have a party, you really should serve *something.*

MICHAEL   We'll make a note.

CHARLES   Are you two all right?

TOM   Sure.

CHARLES   You're the last two left onstage, you know. The ending's up to you. Gay plays end happily now.

Charles heads to the door.

TOM   What about you, Charles, are you going to be okay?

CHARLES   Me? What, you mean . . . ? Oh, yeah. I'm fine. Them's the rules.

Charles exits. Tom turns and looks at Michael in the window. The partying continues down below as the sun sets.

TOM   What am I missing?

MICHAEL   You tell me.

TOM   I'm sorry, Michael. I don't know why I did such stupid things. I love you. But I get distracted. I wish I'd handled it better, the way you did. But I didn't. All I can say is, I'll try to be better. I'll try to . . .

MICHAEL   Stop, please. I didn't hook up with *Joe.* But there were others.

TOM   Others? When? When I was away?

MICHAEL   And when you weren't.

TOM   Oh. That's why Scott knew the way to the bathroom.

Michael doesn't answer.

TOM (*cont.*)   Well, were you safe? I mean, what did you do exactly . . . ?

MICHAEL   I don't feel comfortable talking about this. Are you really that surprised?

TOM   Yes, I am. I thought you didn't like gay men.

MICHAEL   I don't. I just like having sex with them.

TOM   Well, God, okay, so, we're even. It doesn't mean anything.

MICHAEL   Yes, it does. Don't lie—of course it does. And if it doesn't, it should. Stop being so nice and understanding. It makes it too easy to hurt you. Get mad. I am.

TOM (*Anger rising*)   What are you mad about?

MICHAEL   That this is it. We've been playing these stupid roles for everyone to see. Maybe if we had talked about it . . .

TOM   We talk.

MICHAEL   No we don't. We just make jokes and meow.

TOM (*Letting it out*)   Well, you don't make it very easy, you know, always judging me, always making me the bad guy, when all I do is try to make everybody happy.

MICHAEL   Oh, yes, you're a saint.

TOM   No, but I never pretended to be! Shit, I've been working so hard to please everyone—the partners, my mother, my friends. And the only person who doesn't appreciate it is you! I bought you a house!

MICHAEL   You bought that house for us.

TOM   Because you wanted it and I thought it would make you happy. Which was foolish of me because nothing makes you happy. Why is that? How come I make everybody happy but you?

MICHAEL   Maybe you should just make yourself happy, Tom.

Beat.

TOM   Yeah, maybe I should.

MICHAEL   Don't look to me or anybody else for that.

TOM   "Get my needs met."

MICHAEL   Exactly. Exactly. You know something? This is good.

TOM   It is?

MICHAEL   Definitely. We should have done this a long time ago.

TOM   Yeah, I guess so.

MICHAEL   Things will be much easier now. Now we know. We're "glorified roommates." Okay, that's not so bad. I think we'll be okay once we get out of here, you know? Let's just go away. If we could just move to our new house and get away from all of it—the guys, the gym, the plays, the whole parade, we'll be done with it. (*Beat.*)   What do you want to do for dinner? I'm thinking Chinese. Will you order? The usual's fine.

Tom finds a menu in the kitchen. He picks up the phone and dials.

MICHAEL (*cont.*)   That's one thing I'll miss. I'm sure we won't be able to get stuff delivered that fast. Remember the first

98

time we ordered from that place and it seemed like the food arrived before you hung up the phone?

TOM (*Into phone*) Hi, Barry, it's Tom. Can you please call me as soon as you get into the office on Monday? I think we need to cancel the inspection. This isn't going to work. I'll explain. Thanks.

He hangs up.

MICHAEL Tom? What the hell are you doing?

TOM I have to think.

MICHAEL You want to stay in the apartment and keep throwing rent down the drain?

TOM I need some time . . .

MICHAEL Time for what?

TOM Michael, I love you, but this . . . this isn't . . .

MICHAEL Oh, God.

TOM I want more. More than a roommate.

MICHAEL So does everyone. Look out there. And you know something? Compared to most people, I think we're doing pretty well . . .

Tom breaks down and sobs.

TOM I'm sorry, Michael. I'm so sorry.

MICHAEL Don't apologize. (*A touch of panic.*) Okay, um, look, do you want us to see someone? How about that? We'll talk to someone.

TOM I don't know.

MICHAEL   This is not unusual. Really, all couples have problems after seven years. It's the classic, the itch, right? It happens to everyone. In fact, last night in the kitchen, Sherry told me they even went to someone. And now they're doing great. I can get a referral, I'll call her in the morning. Theirs was a straight woman but if you want to go to a gay guy, fine, I'll do that. Every bald guy in Chelsea over forty is a couples therapist. We'll find the right one. There's no reason to panic, we can handle this. Just please, honey, stop crying.

TOM   We haven't had sex with each other in five months.

MICHAEL   We're in a slump, I know that. But, look, we were house hunting, and I had the end of the school year, and you had a bigger caseload. We got very busy . . .

TOM   Five months!

MICHAEL   We lost our connection for a while. We'll get it back.

TOM   I feel you cringe when I go to touch you.

MICHAEL   We'll get it back, Tom.

TOM   I don't think we ever had it.

MICHAEL   Of course we did. We're a good fit, everybody says so.

TOM   That's not the same thing.

MICHAEL   What do you want? Passion? Like you had with James when you were eighteen? Passion fades. Eventually you end up here. God, I can't believe you're going to let that creep ruin everything.

TOM It's not him. I've had this feeling . . .

MICHAEL What feeling?

TOM . . . like it's all passing me by.

MICHAEL What is? What's out there? Tom, take a good look. Those guys are jealous of *us!* They've got fun, hot sex, whatever, but we've got a home. And that's the trade-off. It always is.

TOM It doesn't have to be.

MICHAEL The house was going to be in both our names.

TOM We would figure something out.

MICHAEL How? You're my lawyer.

TOM You'd get another.

MICHAEL How would I pay him? I gave up my job. Did you think of that? I'd be out of work and homeless.

TOM We would figure something out.

MICHAEL So that's it? Seven years and it's all over when you decide? Because you have "a feeling?" I don't understand why you can't at least *try.* There's too much good stuff here. I love you, Tom. And you just said you loved me. Now, maybe that's not enough but it's the right place to start. All I'm asking is that you try. Please, Tom. Say you'll try.

Tom can't. Michael slowly returns to the window.

MICHAEL (*cont.*) I wanted to go to Pottery Barn.

TOM I'm sorry.

MICHAEL   Me, too. I'm sorry, too.

Michael touches his neck and realizes he's still wearing the rainbow beads.

MICHAEL *(cont.)*   I forgot I had these on.

The noise from the street continues. Slow blackout.

END OF PLAY

THE TWILIGHT
OF THE GOLDS

For Mark

The Twilight of the Golds by Jonathan Tolins was presented by Charles H. Duggan, Michael Leavitt, Fox Theatricals, Libby Adler Mages, Drew Dennett, and Ted Snowdon at The Booth Theatre, New York City, on October 21, 1993, with the following cast:

DAVID GOLD	Raphael Sbarge
SUZANNE GOLD–STEIN	Jennifer Grey
ROB STEIN	Michael Spound
PHYLLIS GOLD	Judith Scarpone
WALTER GOLD	David Groh

The Twilight of the Golds was directed by Arvin Brown. The sets were by John Iacovelli, the lighting by Martin Aronstein, the costumes by Jeanne Button, the sound by Jonathan Deans, and Arthur Gaffin was the production stage manager.

The world premiere of *The Twilight of the Golds* was presented by Theatre Corporation of America and Charles H. Duggan at the Pasadena Playhouse in Pasadena, California, on January 17, 1993. The cast and crew were the same with the following exceptions: The role of Suzanne was played by Jodi Thelen. The production was directed by Tom Alderman and the costumes were by Michael Abbott.

TIME

Early autumn through late winter

PLACE

New York

ACT I

SCENE ONE

At rise: the living room of a New York City apartment. It's the home of a young couple and is furnished in the style of a modular catalogue: tasteful, new, not particularly comfortable. A sofa, right, and two armchairs, left, form a triangle center; the left armchair can swivel around. In front of the chairs is a matching hassock which, when topped by a tray, doubles as a coffee table. Upstage left is a hallway that leads to the bedroom. Down right is a trunk with a cushion and down left is a leather reading chair with an ottoman footrest. Next to the reading chair is a small unit with a stereo, CDs, and a three-dimensional replica of a strand of DNA. Medical journals can be seen on the chair and on a side table. Upstage left stands a rolling butcher block on which glasses and an ice bucket sit in preparation for guests.

The only light at first is from the New York City skyline seen through the upstage windows.

DAVID GOLD enters from the hallway and is lit by a spotlight. He addresses the audience and walks downstage.

DAVID   I'm one of those people who takes other people to the opera . . . against their will. I estimate that since the age of fourteen, I've introduced more people to the Met than the good folks at Texaco. And every time, at a performance of *Bohème* or *Aida* or one of the other easy ones, as the chandeliers dimmed, I'd make the same joke. I'd say, "Now, try to enjoy it. It's all right if you don't. You're just here to find out if you have this particular genetic aberration." They usually didn't but they'd look adorable pretending they did.

Anyway, I never imagined how that joke would come back to haunt me. (*He sits on the trunk.*)   I'm a set designer. At least in training. I wanted to design sets for Broadway starting when I was a kid and saw every show in town except *Oh, Calcutta* because you had to be eighteen or older. By the time I was old enough to see *Oh, Calcutta,* Broadway had lost its appeal: hardly any plays, and an audience of nothing but Japanese tourists and Hadassah ladies with husbands who spent the first fifteen minutes of Act One parking the Caddie. So, I embarked on a career in the opera. I'm on the production staff at the Met. Which means I paint a lot of trees. But I figure, if you're going to work in an elitist art form that only a handful of people give a shit about, why not go all the way? And in opera, the composer's dead. So the designer can do something fabulous without getting a pissed-off phone call from Arthur Miller's attorney. For instance . . . (*Lights up on the apartment. David crosses upstage.*)   here we have a smart-looking Manhattan apartment. This is where my sister and her husband lived after they got married. Pages thirty through thirty-four of the Ikea catalogue. No real personality, but nothing objectionable. This is where I saw my family together for the last time. Now, if this were an opera, and everything is, I'd do something spectacular. The Swiss designer, Appia, taught us that a good set is an image of how the characters view the world. Forget what's real, life is too short. (*He sits in the swivel armchair.*)   Take her away.

David spins around and faces upstage. Music: the prelude to Götterdämmerung. *The lighting changes and the rear wall of the living room flies slowly out of sight. Only the wall stage right with the front door remains. We now see the rest of the stage. At the rear and on the sides are huge rocky mountains. Upstage, the other four characters stand on a promontory in silhouette against the sky. The light comes up full as the music reaches its climax and David addresses the audience.*

DAVID   I was in a heavy Wagnerian phase at the time. Immersing myself in the *Ring Cycle* day and night. Pretty impressive, huh? It's a little too *Lost Horizon,* I know, but a lot more interesting than Ikea. This is how I like to picture what happened that stormy season, when I saw the last of the Golds. They would never understand, but to me, it's the perfect setting. Wagner put gods and goddesses on the stage looming on mountaintops in front of stormy skies. With miles of glorious music under them, they decide the fate of the world, not with magic and thunderbolts, but in domestic squabbles: conversations between husband and wife, brother and sister, parent and child.

Upstage, the Gold family join hands and descend from the promontory into the wings.

DAVID (*cont.*)   The Gold family, my nice family, had domestic squabbles and conversations, and we also decided the fate of the world. You'll see.

SUZANNE GOLD-STEIN *enters, turns on a table lamp, and exits left to the kitchen.*

DAVID (*cont.*)   It was my sister's anniversary and we had reservations for dinner. And she had a secret.

He exits through the door. Suzanne reenters carrying a tray with cheese, crackers, and cut vegetables. She stops by the stereo and hits a button. The music changes to soft "party" jazz. She then places the tray down on the hassock and looks at it.

SUZANNE (*Calling off*)   Rob? You know what we need? We need a cheese slicer. I always have to put out a knife. It's very low-class.

ROB STEIN *enters from the kitchen with a bowl of dip which he puts down on the tray.*

ROB It works just as good. Nobody notices.

SUZANNE I can't understand why we don't have one. We must not have registered for it or something. Remind me to steal one the next time we're at my parents' house.

ROB What'll they do when they entertain?

SUZANNE Yeah, right. The last time they "entertained," David and I were brought downstairs at eight-thirty to sing "Matchmaker, Matchmaker" in feetie pajamas. We got paid in Godiva chocolates. (*She looks at the dip.*) What is that?

ROB Dip. I said I'd take care of the dip. This is the dip.

SUZANNE Honey, please tell me that's not Lipton Onion Soup mix and sour cream.

ROB I went to a lot of trouble. I squeezed a lemon.

SUZANNE It's like you're still in junior high school. I'm surprised you don't put out a tray of green M&Ms and tell everybody they make you horny.

ROB (*Grabs her by the waist and pulls her close*) Wanna play "Seven Minutes in Heaven"?

SUZANNE We don't have time.

ROB Suzanne, it's just your parents and your brother.

SUZANNE I'm sorry, but they're important.

ROB I love it when you get that whiny kindergarten voice. It really turns me on.

SUZANNE I'm sorry, but they made me what I am.

ROB Thank God, I thought it was my fault.

SUZANNE Schmuck.

112

They kiss.

ROB Hello.

SUZANNE Hello.

ROB Happy anniversary.

SUZANNE Happy anniversary, Doctor.

ROB (*Looking at the DNA replica*) Do you like the gift we got from Oxy?

SUZANNE Ever so. I always wanted a three-dimensional chromosome in my living room. Why couldn't you work at Tiffany?

She gathers magazines and CDs and puts them away.

ROB Sorry. Dr. Lodge is brilliant but a bit socially challenged. How come we didn't get anything from your office?

SUZANNE Because we're in Chapter Eleven. Can we not talk careers?

ROB (*Takes a small Tiffany gift box from his pocket and prepares to give it to her*) Fine. You want me to open some champagne? We've got some in the fridge.

SUZANNE No, it makes me sleepy.

ROB What are you talking about? It's a special occasion.

SUZANNE I shouldn't drink.

ROB You have your period?

SUZANNE No. And I hate it when you ask me that.

ROB What's eating you?

SUZANNE I just don't want to drink.

The intercom buzzer buzzes. Rob puts the gift back in his pocket and crosses to the front door where he pushes a button on the speaker box. Suzanne puts out coasters.

ROB   Hello?

PHYLLIS   (*Her voice through the intercom*)   Rob? Hi, sweetheart. We made it early, the traffic was light.

ROB   Good, I'll buzz you in.

SUZANNE   Mom?

PHYLLIS   Happy anniversary. Walter's parking the car. There was no traffic.

SUZANNE   I couldn't get an early reservation so we have time to kill.

PHYLLIS   Oh, that's all right. It'll be nice. Oh, you know who I saw at the beauty parlor this afternoon?

ROB   Can this wait till you come up in the elevator?

SUZANNE   Mom, come up.

PHYLLIS   What about your father?

ROB   I can buzz him in when he gets here.

PHYLLIS   Oh. All right. I'll just come up then. Okay.

SUZANNE   Apartment 22B.

Rob presses the buzzer.

SUZANNE   (*cont.*)   Don't be rude. (*She turns off the stereo.*)

Rob shakes his head as he ties his tie.

SUZANNE   (*cont.*)   What?

ROB   Nothing.

SUZANNE *What?*

ROB Nothing. Why are you so nervous around them?

SUZANNE I'm not nervous. I just had a very intense childhood. (*She crosses to him and straightens his tie.*)

ROB Did they beat you?

SUZANNE No. They *loved* me. We're a close family, it's a wonderful thing.

ROB I'm not so sure. Reject your family before they reject you, that's what I always say.

SUZANNE That's horrible. I like your parents. I think it's sweet that they're Orthodox. It gives them that charming, old-world, Amish quality.

The intercom buzzer buzzes. Rob pushes the button.

ROB Hello.

WALTER (*Through the intercom*) Hello?

ROB Hello.

WALTER Yeah, uh, uh, Rob?

ROB Yes.

WALTER Happy anniversary. I don't know what happened to your mother-in-law, I dropped her off.

ROB Yeah, she's on her way up.

SUZANNE Hi, Dad.

WALTER Hi, Suzanne.

The doorbell rings. Rob opens the door for PHYLLIS GOLD, who enters carrying a gift.

WALTER (*cont.*)   We made it here in no time. The traffic was nothing.

PHYLLIS   Your hallway always reeks of garlic, your neighbors must be loud.

ROB   Yeah, just come up.

A siren is heard through the intercom. Phyllis and Suzanne meet center and hug.

WALTER   What? Wait a second, there's an ambulance going by.

SUZANNE   You look good.

PHYLLIS   I'm thinking of having my eyes done. You look stunning. The diet's working.

SUZANNE   This outfit, you can't see.

Suzanne takes Phyllis's wrap off left. Phyllis rearranges the pillows on the sofa.

WALTER   It's amazing, the guys just stopped with the siren still going to buy a pretzel. I'd hate to be the poor *schlub* lying in the back.

ROB   It's a jungle down there. Come up here where it's nice.

PHYLLIS   Is that your father?

WALTER   Phyllis?

PHYLLIS   Walter, I'm up here. They did a good job. The apartment looks gorgeous.

WALTER   I can't wait to see it.

Suzanne reenters.

PHYLLIS   (*Looking out where the windows used to be*)   And the view is stunning. It's clear today, you can see water.

WALTER Really?

ROB (*Desperate*) Why don't I buzz you in?

WALTER Okay.

SUZANNE It's 22B.

WALTER I remember. I'm not your mother.

Rob presses the buzzer.

PHYLLIS (*Crossing to Rob, kissing him*) I nearly got lost in the hall. Hi, Doctor Rob. Happy anniversary. Can you believe it's three years?

ROB No. It feels like we spent twice that on the intercom.

PHYLLIS I could cry. Oh, Rob, I read in the *Times* about those women suing Oxy over unsafe breast implants.

ROB Right. Don't worry about it. Not my department.

PHYLLIS You're not involved?

ROB No, but I'm on the waiting list.

PHYLLIS Oh, thank God. I got scared. But then I thought, Oxy's so big, they must have good lawyers. Here, this is for the two of you. Mazel tov.

Phyllis hands Suzanne the gift and sits. Suzanne sits on the sofa and unwraps the present. Rob pours wine.

SUZANNE Thanks. Nice paper.

ROB Thanks, Mom.

SUZANNE *Uch.* It's still weird when he calls you "Mom." It's like everyone has the same mother or you're all interchangeable.

PHYLLIS   I think it's nice.

ROB   I agree, Mom.

SUZANNE   *Uch.* Stop it. Any minute he's gonna give you his dirty laundry.

PHYLLIS   I wouldn't mind. Did David call?

SUZANNE   He'll be here. (*She takes out the gift: a glass table clock. She and Rob "oooh" together.*)   Ooh, it's pretty. Thanks, Ma.

PHYLLIS   Thank your father.

ROB   Thanks, Mom.

SUZANNE   You have the same one, don't you?

PHYLLIS   Yeah. You always liked it, so I figured it was safe.

The doorbell rings.

SUZANNE   Ma, you're just making it easier for us to turn into you and Dad.

ROB   Your dream.

Rob opens the door. WALTER GOLD *enters, handing his coat to Rob.*

WALTER   Hey there, Rob. Looks like you're holding up pretty good.

ROB   Thanks.

WALTER   (*To Suzanne*)   There she is! (*Kissing her.*)   Hiya, Suzy Q.

SUZANNE   You look fat.

WALTER   Kids. What a pleasure.

SUZANNE We're eating at seven-thirty.

WALTER (*Crossing to the sofa and the food, which he eats continuously*) Fine. Where are we going?

SUZANNE Smith & Wollensky's. You said you wanted steaks.

WALTER Good. That okay with you, Rob?

ROB Whatever you want.

WALTER What, where'd you want to go?

SUZANNE He wanted to go for Thai food on Eighth Avenue.

WALTER You know I can't eat that stuff with my stomach. Besides, it's your anniversary. You don't want to go to some greasy spoon on Eighth Avenue.

ROB I just thought, I don't know, maybe, since it's where I proposed.

PHYLLIS What? You're kidding.

ROB That's where it happened. I put the ring around a piece of chicken satay. Suzanne's hand still smells of peanut sauce.

PHYLLIS That's adorable. Suzanne, why didn't you tell us that story?

SUZANNE I didn't want to give you the ammunition.

WALTER (*Smiling, shaking his head*) That's right. We're so terrible, you really got it rough. (*Looking at the chromosome.*) What the hell is that?

ROB It's a replica of DNA.

PHYLLIS A what?

SUZANNE It's a gift from Oxy.

PHYLLIS It's nice. Where are you putting it?

SUZANNE It's being discussed.

PHYLLIS Whatever—Oh, Denise Kaplan got engaged.

SUZANNE Really?

PHYLLIS To a dentist. Ugly as sin.

SUZANNE Well, she's no beauty. She always had big teeth. Maybe that was the attraction.

PHYLLIS You think she slept with him?

SUZANNE Ma!

WALTER What kind of question is that?

PHYLLIS I'm just wondering.

SUZANNE Of course she did. What are you imagining? She probably gives him great, toothy head.

ROB Suzanne, you're so gross.

WALTER That's the way you talk around your own parents?

SUZANNE (*Smiling*) You can handle it.

PHYLLIS In my day, you didn't do that. Some world. See, years ago, if you got pregnant your life was over. Everyone was so petrified. Now, you have options.

SUZANNE Which is better?

PHYLLIS It's better now, sure. So how early do you think she slept with him?

SUZANNE Ma.

ROB Can we talk about something else?

WALTER Hey, Phyllis, did you tell her who you saw at the beauty parlor?

PHYLLIS Ooh, no. I saw Mrs. Reed.

SUZANNE Really?

ROB Who's that?

SUZANNE My high school biology, physics, and chemistry teacher. She was amazing. That's why I got fives on the APs.

WALTER This dip is delicious.

ROB Thank you. I made it.

WALTER No kidding.

PHYLLIS She always loved you, thought you were the greatest student.

WALTER She was, Rob.

ROB She told me.

PHYLLIS She asked me if you were a surgeon yet. I told her what you were doing.

SUZANNE What'd she say?

PHYLLIS As long as you're happy.

SUZANNE (*Moving away, angry*) Why are you starting?

ROB Don't get upset.

SUZANNE You always have to make me feel bad.

WALTER Sweetheart, your mother didn't mean it like that.

PHYLLIS (*Defensive*) No, she said you were probably smart, that the health-care system is such a shambles, you're better off. Honest.

SUZANNE She was always a snob.

PHYLLIS No, Suzanne, really, she was very down-to-earth. When I said you were a buyer for Bloomingdale's, she asked if you could get her a discount.

SUZANNE You shouldn't tell anyone anything.

ROB What are you so upset about? What are you ashamed of?

WALTER We're all very proud of you.

SUZANNE Will everyone lay off me? I'm not ashamed of anything. I've been out of that school for ten years, I don't care about those people anymore.

WALTER All right. All right.

Pause.

SUZANNE How did she look?

PHYLLIS Good. The same. Teachers don't age.

SUZANNE She'd probably like some of the jewelry we got in. Wait, I'll show you. (*She exits to the bedroom.*)

WALTER Our little girl.

PHYLLIS Did I say anything so terrible? She's so emotional. She gets that from you.

WALTER (*Still eating*) Rob, this dip is sensational.

ROB Thanks, Dad.

SUZANNE (*Entering*) Uch. I wish he'd stop doing that. Here, this is all I have at home.

She hands Phyllis a small jewelry box. Phyllis opens it and takes out a gold ring. Rob joins Walter on the sofa.

PHYLLIS   Oh, this is stunning.

SUZANNE   It's a copy of Paloma Picasso.

PHYLLIS   Really. It's a little like Denise Kaplan's engagement ring.

ROB   That tramp.

PHYLLIS   Walter, look. It's a stunning ring. Fake?

WALTER   Gotta be. Nobody can afford real jewelry anymore. Everybody's dying.

ROB   How's your business?

WALTER   Not bad. Pearson's indestructible. Why? (*Reaching for his wallet.*)   You need money?

ROB   No. Just wondering.

WALTER   We're okay. (*Rising.*)   Pearson will always hang on because we're good at what we do. People give us their money to invest and they use our credit cards because we provide what they're looking for: the appearance if not the reality of financial security.

SUZANNE   Dad, you're scaring me.

WALTER   Don't worry. Phyllis, just keep looking at the fake stuff.

PHYLLIS   (*Still with the ring*)   You think I should get one?

SUZANNE   No, it's cheaply made. See that? That's the trouble with my job, I get too much information about the product. There's always some reason not to buy. It's taken all the fun out of shopping.

ROB   You manage.

PHYLLIS Well, with some things, you just have to go with your feelings.

There is a knock at the door. Suzanne is frightened.

SUZANNE Gimme . . . (*She takes the ring from her mother, puts it back in the case, and places it in a drawer.*)

PHYLLIS What?

WALTER What's the matter?

SUZANNE Shush!

ROB (*Rising*) Honey, maybe it's David.

SUZANNE (*Whispering*) He has a key.

PHYLLIS (*To Rob*) Didn't you pay the rent?

SUZANNE Shh.

There is a tense silence.

DAVID (*Opening the door with his key*) Hello? Anybody home?

SUZANNE David! Oh, thank God it's you.

David enters carrying a small shopping bag. Suzanne hugs him.

DAVID I get that whenever I enter a room. Hi. Happy anniversary. Hi, Mom, Dad. Rob, congratulations. We're counting on you to stick this out.

SUZANNE Shut up. We've got a while before dinner.

DAVID I hope it's Thai. I know a great place on Eighth Avenue.

SUZANNE (*Warning him to drop the subject*) I asked you nice.

WALTER Hey, he looks good.

DAVID Why didn't you open the door when I knocked?

ROB She's just paranoid. David, there are drinks over there.

DAVID (*Crossing to the bar, looking at Walter*) Thanks. You look fat. (*He takes off his coat and pours himself some wine.*)

SUZANNE I'm not paranoid. Three weeks ago, Mrs. Fleischer on the top floor opened her door to see who was knocking and this man burst in and threw her against the wall, screaming at her, calling her a rich bitch.

PHYLLIS That's awful.

SUZANNE He just kept yelling, "You fucking rich bitch, I should kill you."

WALTER Did he take anything?

SUZANNE No. He just smashed stuff. And the weirdest part of it was that he knew the names of everything.

DAVID, PHYLLIS, & WALTER What?

SUZANNE Brand names. He mentioned Waterford crystal, Wedgewood china, and Levolor blinds.

PHYLLIS He has good taste.

DAVID A bit unimaginative. Did he mention Sidney Poitier?

SUZANNE It's not funny.

WALTER Well, you want to move? I thought this was a good neighborhood.

ROB There's no such thing anymore.

SUZANNE We're not gonna move. It's just frightening, that's all.

PHYLLIS Did anyone tell the police?

SUZANNE Yes. They said the best thing to do was not to let anyone in unless they buzzed through the intercom and you know exactly who they are.

DAVID That's neighborly. You'll never meet the people across the hall.

ROB This is New York. You don't actually see your neighbors until they're on the cover of the *Post*.

DAVID Maybe this guy's a messenger, sent to teach us all a lesson about materialism.

SUZANNE Yeah, right. What'd you bring me?

DAVID Ah. The gift of a lifetime.

SUZANNE Gimme.

He takes out a yellow Tower Records bag and removes a boxed set of CDs.

SUZANNE (*cont.*) Oh, not again. I hate it when you do this.

WALTER What is it?

DAVID This is Wilhelm Furtwängler's recording of Richard Wagner's complete *Ring of the Nibelung*. It's the most fascinating work of art man has ever produced. Happy anniversary.

ROB (*Taking the CDs and crossing to the stereo*) Thanks, David. We'll put it with the others.

SUZANNE He always does this. He keeps bringing us CDs of opera and old musicals. It's so rude. He knows we don't have any interest.

DAVID Why are you so closed to everything?

SUZANNE   I'm not closed, I'm discriminating. Just because you like something doesn't mean everyone else has to.

PHYLLIS   Suzanne, try to be appreciative. David, give me a kiss.

David and Phyllis meet center and kiss.

DAVID   You look good, Ma. You shouldn't get any work done.

PHYLLIS   See? He's sweet.

SUZANNE   Fine, you listen to the *Ring of the Niblicks.*

DAVID   I'm just trying to enrich your lives. And I have a friend at Tower, so I get everything real cheap. Someday, you or your children will sit down and listen to this stuff and be transported to new heights.

SUZANNE   Someone, make him stop.

DAVID (*Grandly*)   You know, Suzanne, I think you're afraid. You're afraid of your own soul that hungers for life at a higher pitch.

SUZANNE   Whatever. Thanks.

DAVID   Besides, that's not your real gift. I knew you'd throw a hissy fit. Here. Happy anniversary. (*He pulls a small gift box out of the same bag and hands it to her.*)

SUZANNE   Ooh. What is it?

DAVID   It's a cheese slicer. I didn't think you had one. (*He looks at the knife sticking out of the cheese.*)

SUZANNE   Thank you, we didn't. You're so smart.

Suzanne opens the box and holds the slicer up. The family "oohs." David conducts them louder.

DAVID The handle is crystal. The lady at Fortunoff's said the third anniversary is crystal and glass.

PHYLLIS Oh, I got it right and I didn't even know.

DAVID That's the modern gift. She couldn't remember the traditional. But I figured you're a modern couple.

SUZANNE It's beautiful. I love you. You have the best taste.

DAVID Well, I buy nothing but Wedgewood china and Levolor blinds. Use it in good health.

WALTER So, how ya doin', kiddo? You look great. Doesn't he look great?

PHYLLIS He's too thin.

WALTER He's not too thin. Look at his arms. He's strong. (*He squeezes David's arm.*)

DAVID Well, I've moved up to a heavier drafting pencil.

WALTER So, when are you gonna come play tennis with me?

DAVID Dad, you're a demon on the court. I wouldn't have a chance.

WALTER Rob played with me last weekend.

ROB That's right, Dad.

SUZANNE *Uch.* Cut that out.

DAVID I've been busy. Soon. So, guys, three years, huh? Stephen sends his regards. He would have come but he wasn't invited.

PHYLLIS Now, David, come on, that's not right.

SUZANNE You know you could have brought him. I just thought . . .

WALTER (*Rising*) Hey, what time is it? Rob, do you know what's happening in the game? Is there a TV in your room?

ROB Yeah, sure.

Walter walks with Rob to the bedroom.

WALTER I just gotta check the score.

Pause.

DAVID Sorry.

PHYLLIS Look, that's all right.

DAVID No it's not, I just lost twenty bucks.

SUZANNE You and Stephen make bets on how we'll behave? That's disgusting.

DAVID Hey, I took your side.

PHYLLIS Give it time.

DAVID I know, I know. I'm one of the lucky ones.

PHYLLIS So, how are you, really?

DAVID What? I'm fine.

PHYLLIS Yeah? Then why are you so thin?

SUZANNE You have lost weight, David.

DAVID Will you stop it? Please, I've lost a few pounds. I can't wait for the day when I can lose weight or catch a cold without everyone planning what to read at the memorial.

PHYLLIS Oh, God forbid.

SUZANNE David!

DAVID I'm sorry. I came from a funeral.

SUZANNE Whose?

DAVID A friend of mine, a baritone. Mom, you saw him last year in *The Magic Flute*. With the feathers.

PHYLLIS (*Gasps*) You're kidding. He was gorgeous.

DAVID Don't you know? We all are.

PHYLLIS That's true. They stay young. It's because they don't have children. So he slept around? Mmm.

SUZANNE Stephen could have come.

DAVID Yeah, that's all right. We've been having problems.

SUZANNE Sexual?

PHYLLIS I don't want to hear it. Your generation thinks of nothing but.

DAVID No, not sexual. The sex is fabulous.

PHYLLIS Really? I don't want to hear it.

DAVID It's just tense. He says I force my interests on him.

SUZANNE You?

DAVID He says I'm like a Jewish mother pushing food on a militant anorexic.

He and Suzanne turn to Phyllis.

PHYLLIS What are you looking at me for?

DAVID We're coming up on our third anniversary too.

PHYLLIS Of what?

DAVID Mom, don't be mean. I said you don't need a face-lift. (*Eating a celery stick with Rob's dip.*)   *Uch.* This is Lipton's.

SUZANNE Here, I'll finish it.

PHYLLIS Suzanne, don't eat from his mouth.

SUZANNE Mom. (*Bites the other end of the celery stick and puts the rest away in a napkin.*)

PHYLLIS So, what, are you gonna break off with him?

DAVID I hope not. I really can't face dating again. I feel lonely sometimes.

SUZANNE I worry about you.

DAVID I know you do.

SUZANNE We should go out more, the four of us.

DAVID I know we should. But Stephen thinks Rob is homophobic.

SUZANNE He is not. Just because his parents think you're an abomination doesn't mean he does.

DAVID Thank you.

SUZANNE People don't automatically think the way their parents do. It's not fair to . . .

DAVID Suzanne, don't worry about it. Stephen thinks everybody is homophobic, including me. So, what about you, Anniversary Girl? How's it going?

SUZANNE I'm good. We're good.

DAVID Yeah?

SUZANNE Yeah.

DAVID I'm glad.

PHYLLIS It's so beautiful the way you two get along. I'm *kvelling*. I guess I did something right.

SUZANNE Mom, you did everything right.

PHYLLIS Yeah, sure.

SUZANNE I've got a surprise.

DAVID What?

SUZANNE An announcement. Big one. Rob doesn't know.

DAVID You little minx. What is it?

PHYLLIS Oh, thank God, you're going back to medical school.

SUZANNE No. And why do you have to say things like that?

DAVID Mother, behave or we'll put you in a home.

Walter and Rob enter, talking baseball.

WALTER Lousy Mets. Same thing every year.

ROB They'll be back.

WALTER It's so aggravating.

DAVID Dad, we should go to a game together. When's helmet day?

WALTER You hate baseball.

DAVID I do. But I love those little helmets.

PHYLLIS How's your job, David?

SUZANNE Are you making any money?

DAVID Suzanne, I'm an artist.

WALTER That means no.

DAVID Don't worry about me. I'm working my way up in an art form that is dearly loved by very rich people.

WALTER Just hope they can hold on to their money.

DAVID That's your job, Dad.

PHYLLIS What are you working on now?

SUZANNE Mom, don't get him started.

DAVID Wagner's *Ring Cycle,* day and night.

SUZANNE I thought he was an anti-Semite.

DAVID That's a simplification. Wagner might have had Jewish blood.

PHYLLIS Jewish anti-Semites, they're the worst.

ROB What's it about?

SUZANNE Oh, God. Wake me up when it's over.

PHYLLIS Suzanne, listen to your brother.

WALTER You'll like this, it's about jewelry. It's about a gold ring that everybody fights for. And for that you gotta sit for a week.

DAVID Twenty-two hours with intermissions.

ROB That's worse than Rosh Hashanah.

WALTER Nothing's worse than Rosh Hashanah.

DAVID And it's not about a ring. Not just a ring. It's about everything. Life, love, civilization, evolution. It's amazing. This twisted little anti-Semite with bad skin and BO created a work of art that is as unfathomable as the Bible.

WALTER He talks so dramatic.

133

DAVID   Let me give you an example. The last scene of *Die Walküre*. Wotan, the head god, is angry at his daughter, Brünnhilde, because she defied his wishes.

ROB   What'd she do?

DAVID   If I answer that, we'll never eat. Just go with me. Brünnhilde is Wotan's favorite child, she is the living embodiment of his will.

PHYLLIS   He speaks so beautifully, doesn't he? Remember in junior high . . .

DAVID   Ma! But she has disobeyed him. Wotan has no choice but to punish her by taking away her godhead.

SUZANNE   Her what?

DAVID   He makes her a mortal woman. He puts her to sleep and lays her down on a rock surrounded by magic fire. Brünnhilde will rest there until a hero brave enough to walk through that fire can wake her.

As he speaks, the sky behind him starts to flicker and then becomes engulfed with beautiful red flames. This is the "magic fire" and the music from this scene can be heard softly in the background.

DAVID (*cont.*)   A hero who knows nothing of fear and obeys only Nature's law. A hero who is strong enough and courageous enough to truly love. Wotan knows too well that he will never see his child again. He kisses her on the forehead and says, "Farewell, you valiant, glorious child!" Forced into obeying laws that he no longer understands or believes in, this god must abandon what he loves most of all. In one moment, with fire sweeping through the sky, we see parent and child, god and mortal, parting ways for eternity. And we know that it could be no other way.

The fire and music fade away. Pause.

PHYLLIS Doesn't he speak beautifully?

SUZANNE When he explains it, it sounds interesting.

WALTER Meanwhile, it takes five and a half hours to get to that scene.

DAVID Nine if you count *Rheingold.*

ROB We should go. See it once.

SUZANNE Have fun. I would never make it, I slept through *Dances with Wolves.* Either that or I'd start laughing uncontrollably like Mary at Chuckles's funeral.

DAVID "A little song, a little dance . . ."

SUZANNE & DAVID ". . . a little seltzer down your pants."

They laugh together.

ROB What are you talking about?

WALTER What is that?

DAVID & SUZANNE *Mary Tyler Moore Show.*

SUZANNE When Chuckles the Clown dies, and Mary can't stop laughing at his funeral.

WALTER Eighty thousand dollars in education between them and they still communicate through sitcom reruns. Can you imagine?

PHYLLIS (*Still hooked*) How does it end, David? I don't remember?

DAVID The *Ring?*

SUZANNE Ma, wasn't one bad enough?

PHYLLIS   Come on, tell us. I'm interested.

DAVID   Very simple. The end of everything as we know it. The world has become corrupt and lazy. It seems that mortals lie, cheat, and steal even worse than the gods did. True love is destroyed as people cling to twisted ideas of honor and duty that are based on lies. Brünnhilde's hero, Siegfried, is murdered. Inconsolable, and seeing how the world is turning to shit, she erects a giant funeral pyre.

He rises. Again, the flames appear faintly in the sky behind him and we hear the music from the "immolation scene."

DAVID (*cont.*)   There is no point in preserving this failed civilization. Brünnhilde sacrifices herself and all that is in the hope that something better may emerge. She calls up to Wotan, sitting powerless in his castle in the sky, *"Ruhe, ruhe, du Gott!"* Rest, rest, O God! She mounts her horse and jumps into the fire. The flames rise to consume everything in sight, including the castle of the gods. (*The image of water replaces the flames.*)   And then, the mighty river overflows its banks and sweeps away all the wreckage, covering everything and everyone with a great flood of rebirth and new potential. Finally, as the water sinks back to its natural level, a few dazed survivors appear to behold the brave new world that stands before them. It's up to them now. And it's up to us what to make of it.

The water image disappears. The music fades away. There is a slight pause.

PHYLLIS   Beautiful.

DAVID   That's just a rough idea. There's a lot more to it than that. I left out the dragon and the dwarfs. You can see how it's fun to work on.

WALTER   What was that German?

DAVID   *"Ruhe, ruhe, du Gott."* Rest, rest, God, your work is done.

WALTER   Here translate this: *"Es, es, shane, Gott im Himmel."* *Faschtaste?*

DAVID   I only speak opera German. What does it mean?

WALTER   It's Yiddish for "Eat, eat, for God's sake!" Can we go yet?

SUZANNE   Just a few more minutes. We're not getting there early so you can *schmooze* the maître d'. (*She starts to clear the food away.*)

ROB   David, you know, it sounds really interesting.

SUZANNE   It does?

ROB   We talk about this stuff constantly at Oxy.

DAVID   Opera?

ROB   No, of course not. No, the idea of a postnatural epoch. We talk about the role of our research in evolutionary history. What *we* do now that God is resting.

PHYLLIS   He's either resting or in a coma.

ROB   We're very close to releasing some historic technology.

WALTER   I'm glad to hear it. Thank God.

DAVID   Why are you so happy?

WALTER   I bought some Oxy stock. Biotechnology is a big field. You've got to watch health trends. You know, I could have bought shares in a company making condoms in 1983—didn't take it. Can you imagine, with all that's happened? Can you imagine?

SUZANNE Dad, that's sick.

ROB Why? Look, if lives are saved, it's okay if somebody makes a buck.

WALTER Exactly.

ROB The government isn't helping anymore. So now, whatever we come up with in the labs has to be something with profit potential. Which also means we have to be protective of any discoveries. That's what's holding up the new big thing.

DAVID What's the "new big thing"?

ROB I'm not supposed to talk about it.

DAVID You just did.

ROB I really shouldn't.

SUZANNE David, you don't want him to lose his job.

DAVID Come on. What, I'm going to steal Oxy Co.'s big discovery and start cloning people in my kitchenette? I'm just interested in the abstract.

ROB All right. But it's not to leave this room. It looks like the Human Genome Project is a lot further along than everybody thinks.

PHYLLIS Really. What's that?

ROB Basically, what I'm saying is that we've finally developed advanced procedures for individual gene identification. Including a way to do these tests through amniocentesis at the end of the first trimester.

DAVID Which means?

138

ROB The possibilities are endless. Think about it. This is an unbelievable breakthrough. It opens new doors. Unfortunately, it will be a while before the public knows about it, because, typically, we're fighting in court over the patents.

WALTER Patents? On the equipment?

ROB On the genes.

DAVID You still didn't answer my question. What does it mean?

ROB What, you mean practical applications?

DAVID That'd be good.

SUZANNE Don't be snotty.

ROB Curing genetic diseases for one. There are people walking around with these ticking time bombs in their DNA waiting to go off. By locating the gene, we're ten times closer to a cure.

PHYLLIS I had a friend, remember Gloria Myers? Her mother had Huntington's.

ROB Perfect example.

PHYLLIS I used to go to her house. Her mother couldn't walk or eat by herself. She kept having these hysterics, wanting to speak, to communicate somehow, and just being defeated by her body. Finally, she gave up.

WALTER Terrible thing.

PHYLLIS And everywhere you looked in that house there were reminders of what she was like before. Pictures, paintings the mother used to do, the piano she used to play.

I knew it was killing Gloria. Not only seeing her mother fall apart that way, but knowing that the same thing could happen to her. Can you imagine, feeling like you're looking at your own future that way? Just awful, her mother. You've never seen anyone look so terrible.

DAVID I have.

A short pause.

SUZANNE How is Gloria? What happened to her?

PHYLLIS We lost touch. I don't remember why.

WALTER Very sad.

DAVID (*Back to business*) There's more to it, isn't there?

ROB What do you mean?

DAVID All that genetic decoding. That's dangerous stuff.

WALTER What dangerous? Is anybody else starving to death?

ROB Sure, there are going to be ethical questions. Who is privy to the information? The insurance companies? The government? Things like that will be argued case by case until we can come up with some sort of standards.

DAVID What about the amniocentesis?

ROB What about it?

DAVID Why'd you mention it? What are you going to do with it?

ROB Simple. By having the information available before birth, you'll determine what problems or abnormalities may be present in the fetus. Doctors can be ready for any emergencies. And the parents can be trained to help the child overcome any behavioral predispositions.

WALTER We could have taught Suzanne to hate shopping.

ROB Later on, by using this information, we can develop ways to correct or reverse the genes.

PHYLLIS Maybe they could give me a sense of direction.

ROB That's years away. Until then, in tragic scenarios, the parents and doctors may choose to terminate the pregnancy.

DAVID On what grounds?

ROB I told you. At first, as with anything, it will be on a case by case basis.

DAVID I don't believe this. Do you people have any idea how dangerous this is?

SUZANNE I thought you were pro-choice.

ROB Look, David, we are, in effect, on the verge of creating a better world. That's what science is—the pursuit of a better world, one that minimizes misery.

DAVID Whose? Face it, Rob, this is eugenics. It's blatant Nazi philosophy.

ROB Oh, here we go. Every time there's the slightest scientific advance, some knee-jerk liberals start shouting about Nazis. We are trying to make life better. You should hear Dr. Lodge speak. He's truly eloquent on the subject.

DAVID Lodge? Dr. Adrian Lodge?

ROB You know him?

DAVID I saw him on *Nightline*.

PHYLLIS He's very distinguished.

DAVID For a Nazi.

ROB   The man is at the top of his field.

DAVID   Rob, how can you buy into this? You're a Jew. Your parents are Orthodox, for God's sake.

ROB   Yes, I'm a Jew, so I'm wary of political evil masquerading as science. Absolutely. But I don't see politics here.

DAVID   Oh, come on.

ROB   And, as a Jew, I believe in the value of knowledge, the rewards of study. Period.

SUZANNE   Is this really how we want to spend our anniversary?

ROB   Knowledge is neutral. It simply is. It's what bad people do with that knowledge that's dangerous.

DAVID   It's good people that scare me.

ROB   David, do me a favor. Imagine a world without Huntington's disease. One where that woman's mother can still play the piano. That's what we're working towards. A world without needless suffering.

DAVID   Okay, I get it. I imagine a world without critics.

ROB   I'm being serious.

DAVID   So am I. I imagine a world without critics. A brave new world without John Simon. But then that's also a world without George Bernard Shaw. You can't lose one without the other.

WALTER   Have you been to the theater lately? We already live in a world without George Bernard Shaw.

PHYLLIS   Someone at the beauty parlor was talking about women who had abortions because they found out they were having girls and they wanted boys.

DAVID   What about that?

ROB   A world with more boys, you'd love that.

SUZANNE   Rob, don't.

Pause; David smiles. Rob turns away, embarrassed.

DAVID   Well, yeah, maybe I would. But it's not our place to create. We have enough problems of our own.

ROB   You don't under—

PHYLLIS (*Stands and interrupts the argument*)   I have faith in people. They'll make the right decision most of the time. Especially in this country. On the whole, I think people are good.

WALTER   Aww, isn't that beautiful?

DAVID   Yes. Thank you, Anne Frank.

PHYLLIS   Fine, make fun of me. But I mean it. I believe in the family of man.

DAVID   What about our friend who likes to smash Wedgewood china and yell at Mrs. Fleischer?

PHYLLIS   If given a chance, an education, and love, he could come home to the family of man.

WALTER   I'm getting the coats. (*Exits to the bedroom.*)

ROB   Look, David, I understand how you feel. Sometimes I wish we could get out of the way and let Nature take over, like in the opera. But in reality, Nature fails. You have no idea what horrific defects can strike a person, and now we can find out before they embark on a tragic life. We have the technology, we're going to have more and more information. There's no going back. Why force someone

143

through an unhappy existence? Not to mention their family. Let's give people the choice. Let each family do what's right. It's nobody else's business, not the government's, not some religious crackpot's, not even the doctor's. (*Crossing to David.*)   Just last week, a woman at New York Hospital found out that her fetus had a tumor the size of a baseball on the tailbone. If it was benign, the doctors would have to remove it and the kid would have no legs or backside. If it was malignant, the kid would die. That's Nature, David. That's God's work, but now we have the ability to head it off at the pass.

Suzanne cries out, obviously agitated. Walter reenters with the coats. Phyllis and David cross to her.

SUZANNE   Oh, God, can we please stop this? I can't take it anymore. This conversation is so horrible.

WALTER   What?

PHYLLIS   Suzanne, what is it?

ROB   Suzanne?

DAVID   You need a drink?

SUZANNE   No. I'm pregnant.

A slight pause. And then, the scene is transformed to one of complete joy. Phyllis screams with delight. As the Golds hug one another and celebrate, Rob slowly sits down on the trunk.

PHYLLIS   I knew it! You said you had a surprise. I didn't want to jinx it!

WALTER   My little girl! Congratulations, Rob.

DAVID   Well, it's about time. I was born to be an uncle.

ROB When did you find out?

SUZANNE Yesterday.

ROB And you didn't tell me?

SUZANNE I wanted to tell everybody together at dinner. But then, I got so upset with all that talk about . . .

PHYLLIS (*Rushing over and covering Suzanne's ears*) No, don't think about it, don't think about it, don't think about it.

DAVID Congratulations, Sis.

WALTER Hey, speaking of dinner, come on, let's go already.

They prepare to leave.

SUZANNE Are you happy, Rob?

The others turn to hear his reply.

ROB Of course I am. Are you crazy?

WALTER Hey, Rob, you want to call your parents before we leave?

ROB No, it's the Shabbas, they won't answer the phone.

PHYLLIS Oh, that's a shame. This is such a beautiful moment.

WALTER That's right, Grandma.

PHYLLIS Shut up.

WALTER This is what life is all about. The family together, everybody healthy, good news to share.

DAVID (*Joining his parents in an embrace*) We're very lucky people.

WALTER That's for sure. When this goes, we're really in trouble. Come on. (*Walter ushers Phyllis out the door.*)

ROB We're late.

DAVID You know, Stephen's and my anniversary is in six months. So, I guess you'll all be at our house.

SUZANNE (*On her way out*) David!

DAVID Who knows? Maybe I'll be pregnant.

They are gone except for Rob who lingers for a moment. Suzanne enters downstage right from the wings, watching the scene. Rob puts on his coat, gathers his strength and follows the others out.

SCENE TWO

Suzanne addresses the audience:

SUZANNE I should have told him first. "Shoulda, woulda, coulda." Do you get points for at least knowing when you should have done something? Do I get partial credit for guilt? I should have stayed in ballet class. I should have invited Margo the handicapped girl to my bat mitzvah. I should have been a doctor. That's a biggie. I had the interest, had the grades. But I hate being tested. My heart starts pounding and my hands sweat. You can't get an MD if you hate being tested, so I switched to marketing. My parents were devastated. They said I always take the easy way out. I guess I do, I married Rob. No, I take that back. There's nothing wrong with Rob. My name was Gold, his was Stein, if I married him I'd be Goldstein, it made Jewish sense. You should have seen him in college. Rob was amazing, really passionate about everything, like he didn't know it was the eighties. When he chose research over a

146

medical practice, I thought it was so noble, so sexy. I didn't think how much less he'd be making than the average anesthesiologist. I take that back, too. God, why do I do that? I love Rob. I couldn't live without him. I tried. Five years ago. We had been together *forever* and I decided enough was enough. I needed to find myself and reach my potential. Dr. Rob was a symbol of everything wrong with my life. So, I walked. It was exhilarating at first. On-the-go in the big city. Got a new outlook, a new self-image. I was ready to start dating. (*Beat.*)   *Uch,* how do people do this? I would go with women from work to bars and then go home and cry my eyes out. I'm sorry, I am not equipped to sit in some yuppie watering hole with my tits sticking out and appear interested in some MBA with thinning hair telling Ivan Boesky jokes. But, I didn't give up. I took control of my life and I went, I swear to God, to a computer dating service. Data Dates. On Lexington. Isn't that embarrassing? I met with this perky woman named Jan who still had a Dorothy Hamill haircut which I thought was rather odd. She told me they have a large base of subscribers who pay yearly until they find their "life mate"—that's what she said: "life mate." It sounded like something on *Nova*. They take down all this information and then they put you on a video. There's a library that has books of pictures of the people available and then you can watch the ones who interest you on TV. "Well, Jan, that sounds very high-tech," I said, which made her even perkier. "Oh, Suzanne, I really want to see this work for you. Are you committed? Tell me you are and we'll get started right away." It was very seductive, you know, in a Jews for Jesus kind of way. And then I asked about the money. "Suzanne, don't let the money stop you. We'll work it out." "But, how much is it?" Okay, it was thirty-five hundred dollars for the first six months and twenty-two fifty after that. I said, "Excuse me?" And then Jan tossed her Dorothy Hamill hair to one side and said, "I know it sounds like a lot. Let me talk to my supervisor." By this point, my heart was pounding like during the SAT's, so I slipped out of Jan's office and ran down the hall to the elevator. And there on the left was the library. I knew I wasn't supposed to go in, I wasn't "committed," but I couldn't resist, I had to see. I opened the eligible-man book and tried not to hyperventilate. (*Beat.*) How can I describe to you what I saw? The best I can do is: Think of the most revolting blind date you've ever had. He would be the cute one. God, how dare these people take advantage of our needs that way. Especially in a desperate era like this one. I ran home and cried my eyes out. Were these really my options—whining Wharton graduates or "dating cults"? Or being alone? It was multiple choice and I never felt so unprepared. I just wanted to crawl under a rock and go to sleep for thirty years. I called Rob immediately.

Rob enters through the front door.

SUZANNE (*cont.*)   Two months later, we were engaged.

Lights up on the apartment. Rob looks out the door, saying good-bye to the Golds.

ROB   No, the elevator's that way, Mom.

PHYLLIS (*Offstage*)   They're still with the cooking next door.

ROB   David, grab your mother. Good night.

The Golds ad-lib "good nights" as Rob closes and triple-locks the door.

SUZANNE   You're mad.

ROB   Why didn't you tell me? How could you not tell me?

SUZANNE   I thought it would be nice if you all found out together.

ROB   I can't believe you. You're having a child with your husband. You acted like you were bringing home your report card! I felt like I was totally out of the loop. You didn't even look at me when you said it. I was waiting for your father to ask me what my involvement was. It was humiliating.

SUZANNE   I thought we would celebrate now, just the two of us, but I guess that's out of the question.

ROB   Just this once, Suzanne, I should have been more important. You're going to have to decide, once and for all—it's them or me. I am sick of being married to Brenda Potemkin.

SUZANNE   Who?

ROB   The spoiled princess in *Goodbye, Columbus.*

SUZANNE   That's my parents' favorite movie.

ROB   No kidding.

SUZANNE   Rob, stop it. You are the most important person in my life. I live with you, don't I?

ROB   That's not enough and you know it.

SUZANNE (*Crosses to him and kisses him*)   I promise. You can have my undivided attention up until the baby is born.

ROB   I'm doomed.

SUZANNE   I love you.

They kiss. He softens and takes her in his arms.

SUZANNE (*cont.*)   Rob?

ROB What?

SUZANNE Do you think we're ready for this?

ROB More than most. Yeah. I think in some ways, it's just what we need.

SUZANNE Me too.

ROB If it will make you happy for once.

SUZANNE The timing is right, don't you think?

ROB I guess.

SUZANNE I think it's a good time. The apartment is finished. (*Looking around.*) Well, close enough.

ROB It looks fine.

SUZANNE So, what are you hoping for? Boy or girl? I can't wait to find out so we can start painting.

ROB We don't have to.

SUZANNE What?

ROB We don't have to wait. I can talk to Dr. Lodge. We can get an amniocentesis at Oxy. The new one.

SUZANNE God. Really?

ROB We should test for Tay-Sachs anyway.

SUZANNE Isn't it too early?

ROB No. Not for us. Adrian is always saying we need more subjects for study. We can do it in a couple of weeks. Consider it a perk. Which is another reason you should have told me first.

SUZANNE I'm sorry.

ROB God forbid there's anything wrong, we could have taken care of it without everybody knowing. Now, God forbid, it would be a mess.

SUZANNE Rob, are you crazy? You think I could go through something like that without telling my parents?

ROB No, of course not. You can't fart without telling your parents.

SUZANNE Rob! Why are you being so mean to me? I'm a pregnant woman, I'm not in my right mind. I'm very fragile!

ROB Is this what I have to look forward to?

SUZANNE I'm in hormone hell.

ROB I always thought pregnant women were really sexy.

SUZANNE Yeah? You want to do something about it?

ROB Maybe. But shouldn't you call your folks first?

SUZANNE No. They're not home yet. Rob, I was scared. I wanted to rally the troops.

ROB You don't have to, you know that. If you just let me in . . .

SUZANNE I know.

ROB We're gonna be fine. This is a good thing.

SUZANNE You mean it?

ROB I'm telling you.

SUZANNE I don't call my parents when I fart.

ROB Uh-huh.

He pulls the Tiffany gift box from his pocket and gives it to her. Suzanne gasps and buries her head in his chest. He leads her toward the bedroom as Walter enters from the wings downstage left and watches them.

ROB   Can I talk to Dr. Lodge? He'll be more than happy to do it.

SUZANNE   It's so frightening. Maybe we should wait.

ROB   Look, I'm sure it's okay. Why take a chance? It's just information.

They exit.

SCENE THREE

Walter addresses the audience:

WALTER   I went to the doctor the other day because my stomach was being a little too sensitive to the Dow Industrial Average. Sometimes I think they should use my bowel movements as a major economic indicator. Anyway, I was stuck sitting in the waiting room—amazing how those guys get away with that—and I started reading one of those *People*-type magazines. They had a ten-page spread on all these Hollywood stars who are coming out now and saying they were physically and emotionally abused by their parents. Can you imagine? My mother is seventy-eight years old, I would be afraid to say something like that in private, never mind in a magazine. She would come to my office and bash my head in with a frozen noodle pudding. And I'm telling you, she was worse than any of them. We just didn't think in those terms. We didn't spend our lives trying to figure out how many ways our parents screwed us up. They managed to make it through Depression and war keeping food on the table and clothes on our back, and if they didn't say "I love you" once a week or give you enough "positive reinforcement," you lived. America made too much money, that's the problem. Suddenly, we got all this time to sit around and figure out why we're still not happy. You notice it's movie stars and yuppies who go on *Donahue* and into therapy to talk about their rotten parents. Your average guy making ends meet doesn't give a rat's ass about "getting in touch with the child within." He wants to get fed and he wants to get laid. Done. Blaming their parents, the nerve of them. When we were growing up, it was the kids who were the disappointments. Is that out of fashion now, or what? (*Pause.*)   I can't say these things around Phyllis or she'll give me the look. You know the look. The one that says, "All right, I love you anyway." I hate that look. It doesn't even take long for it to work, maybe half a second and I crumble inside. Because there it is, the face of the woman I've lived with for thirty years saying that I don't deserve her, which I know is true, or that I don't love the kids as much as she does, which I know she thinks, but which is utter nonsense. I love my kids so much I want to burst. Just look at them. They're smart, smarter than Phyllis and me ever were. They've got a rhythm when they talk, it's amazing, you can't keep up. They're beautiful. But, look, I'm disappointed. Sure. Every parent has been disappointed by their children since God with Adam and Eve. (*Beat.*)   Suzanne, she could have been a doctor, a surgeon yet. She had straight A's. But she likes to take the easy way out. So she works at Bloomingdale's, a place, thank God, that hasn't gone under. Yet. She married early, the first guy she went with seriously. The first guy. Still, Rob's good to her, I can't complain. And David? Oh, he could have been . . . he could have been anything he wanted to be. On television, if he wanted. With everything

153

we did for him . . . But, that's life. What are you gonna do? You give your life for them, they disappoint you, and you love them. And that's the gift. You find yourself able to love them, even with all the crap. They didn't ask to come into this world. It was our decision. You throws the dice, you takes your chances. And you try not to think about it.

Lights up on the apartment. Suzanne enters at the end of Walter's speech. She is talking on the phone.

SUZANNE No. I won't show for at least another month, I think. Okay, what? No way. We are not calling it David. Because you're not dead, that's why. It's spooky. I don't care what gentiles do. David . . . Yeah? Okay, what if it's a girl? Davida? Davida Stein? She'd end up planting trees in the Golan Heights. You're crazy.

ROB (*Enters the apartment with a briefcase*) Hi.

She waves to him and continues on the phone. Rob goes through the day's mail.

SUZANNE Now you're really pushing it. There's no way we're going to name our firstborn Siegfried. David, I have to go, Rob just got home. You get back to work. Make some money, we're all ashamed of you. I'm kidding. God. Okay, bye. (*She hangs up and kisses Rob.*)

SUZANNE Hi. I think David is more anxious than we are.

ROB I heard.

SUZANNE Honey, I know this sounds ridiculous, but this afternoon, I think I felt like a kick. Not a kick, maybe, more like a knock. Like, "Hello, I'm in here." It was incredible.

ROB That's impossible. It's too early. There's no way.

SUZANNE   What's the matter?

ROB   Sit down, we have to talk.

SUZANNE   Oh no. Oh no. Oh, God. Oh, God. It's deformed, isn't it? It has no arms or it's blind or—what? Oh, God. Oh, God. Oh, God.

ROB (*Overlapping*)   No, no, no. No. Calm down, please, will you? It's nothing like that.

SUZANNE   Well, what?

ROB   Sit down. Let's go through it.

Rob leads her to a chair. He then takes out a folder from his briefcase and sits next to her. He removes some computer printouts from the folder and lays them out in front of them.

SUZANNE   My hands are sweating.

ROB   Okay. Dr. Lodge was very pleased with how it went. He was able to get a good sampling of the genetic material and all the tests were completed. Now remember, we're still in an experimental area. I mean, they can't guarantee that this information is 100 percent accurate.

SUZANNE   Will you just tell me?

ROB   Okay. It's a boy. No physical deformities.

SUZANNE   Ten fingers, ten toes?

ROB   Ten fingers, ten toes.

SUZANNE   Ten fingers and toes. Well, what then? Is it retarded?

ROB   No. As a matter of fact, it looks like it will be quite intelligent. Probably left-handed.

155

SUZANNE   Yeah? So . . . what? What?

ROB   It will probably be like David. (*A beat.*)   We matched the chromosomes from the test with the data compiled in the computer and found the presence of those genes that we've statistically linked to that trait. Then, to double-check what we detected, we examined the magnetic image that we made of the brain. And, sure enough, the size of the hypothalamus is much smaller than the average, even at this early stage of development. Also, the anterior commissure connecting the cortex of the right and left sides of the brain is significantly larger than normal. Those are both in accordance with the latest studies. All of this information taken together has led Dr. Lodge to that conclusion.

SUZANNE   Oh.

ROB   He estimates it's 90 percent certain. But he has a big ego, so who knows? Still, the evidence suggests that that's what we've got.

Pause.

SUZANNE   What do we do?

ROB   I don't know.

SUZANNE   They could be wrong.

ROB   Yes. That's a definite possibility. And it's not like we can point to one gene and say "aha." It's the whole composite of evidence that's open to interpretation.

SUZANNE   So, it could be a mistake.

ROB   Adrian says 90 percent sure. I believe him.

SUZANNE   Can we pretend we never heard this?

ROB   Can *you*?

SUZANNE (*Thinks a moment, then*)   No. Will any kid we have . . . ?

ROB   That's very unlikely. There are cases of siblings, but almost never all of them.

SUZANNE   What about environment? I mean if we know before, couldn't we raise it in a way that . . .

ROB   It's possible, but who knows how? And judging by how clearly it shows up in the statistical evidence, we'd have a lot of nature to nurture against. But, yes, I guess we could try something like that if you want.

SUZANNE   I tried to think of everything. All my life, I've tried to visualize bad things really clearly so they wouldn't happen, because things never happen when you expect them. But I never thought of that. I didn't know they could . . .

ROB   Well, we can.

SUZANNE   Are you mad at me?

ROB   Of course not. What a stupid thing to say.

SUZANNE   But he's my brother.

ROB   It's nobody's fault. That's just the way it is.

SUZANNE   But you're upset.

ROB   I'm not thrilled.

SUZANNE   How can you be sarcastic?

ROB   I'm answering your question. Yes, I'm upset.

SUZANNE (*Softly*)   We could get rid of it. I mean . . .

Beat.

ROB We could. Yes. We could . . .

SUZANNE (*Tentative*) I don't *want* to . . .

ROB I know. Sure.

SUZANNE I mean, it's not something I ever thought I'd have to do.

ROB No. It would have to be considered very carefully.

SUZANNE God. How . . . ?

ROB We don't have to decide tonight.

SUZANNE No, of course not.

ROB But, you don't want to take too much time with that decision. The earlier the better.

SUZANNE Right. I know. Oh, God. What do other people do?

ROB What do you mean?

SUZANNE I mean, what's the precedent?

ROB There is no precedent. It's just us. I'm going to get out of this suit. (*He walks to the bedroom.*)

SUZANNE If only it were deformed.

ROB Suzanne!

SUZANNE It wouldn't be so complicated, that's all. This is so complicated.

ROB We'll be okay. (*He exits.*)

Suzanne sits still for a moment. She then picks up the telephone and presses the speed-dial button.

SUZANNE (*Into phone*)   Mom? It's me. Don't get hysterical.

Rob appears in the hallway and looks at Suzanne. Music: the "Forest Murmurs" from Siegfried.

End of Act I

ACT II

Music: "The Ride of the Valkyries." The lights reveal David upstage center in dramatic silhouette against the sky. He walks downstage and cuts the music off abruptly with his arms.

DAVID   Oh, sure, everybody knows that part. That's "The Ride of the Valkyries." I nearly got in a fist fight with an usher who referred to it as "Theme from *Apocalypse Now*." These things are important to me. (*He sits*.)   At the end of *Götterdämmerung,* Brünnhilde returns the magic ring to the river Rhine, from where it was stolen in the first place. And right after she does this, the world ends in a cataclysm of fire and water. Now, since the first performance, people have pointed out that doesn't make any sense. We're told over and over that all the trouble started when the gold was stolen from its natural place in the Rhine, so when it's put back, the curse should end and everybody should live happily ever after. The gods don't have to die, the world doesn't have to burn, we don't have to start all over. So why does it happen? Wagner went through a slew of different endings and this is the one he decided upon, he must have known what he was doing, there must be a simple explanation. And there is. When a friend asked him why it happens this way he said, "Listen to the music, you'll know." And sure enough, the arrogant little Nazi was right. You sit in the theater and experience this onslaught of sound and destruction, and you know that it was all inevitable. This is the way everything comes to an end. I find myself in the same position when I tell friends about what happened to the Golds. They say, "I don't believe it," or "That makes no sense." And the only explanation I can give is, "If you were there, you'd know."

Logic is beside the point. I think that's why I love the opera. When art is at its most outrageous, when it cannot be easily believed, that is when it most resembles life. The answers are in the experience.

David snaps his fingers. Music: "The Valhalla Theme" from Das Rheingold. *The apartment slides upstage and is replaced by the kitchen of Phyllis and Walter's suburban home. A swinging door leads to the rest of the house. There's a table with two chairs right and a counter with two tall stools left. Phyllis stands by the counter with an urgent expression on her face.*

DAVID (*cont.*)   My mother called me to the house one Sunday to help her with an urgent problem.

Lights up full as David joins Phyllis. The music fades out.

PHYLLIS   One more time, please.

DAVID   All right. The TV and the VCR always stay on channel three.

PHYLLIS   Always?

DAVID   Always.

PHYLLIS   What if . . .

DAVID   *Always.* But the cable box can go to any station you want. Now repeat what I just said.

PHYLLIS   Repeat?

DAVID   Repeat.

PHYLLIS & DAVID   The TV and the VCR *always* stay on channel three, but . . .

PHYLLIS   Wait, wait, this is the hard part—but the cable box can go to any station you want. Oh, okay.

DAVID   You and Dad are really pathetic.

PHYLLIS   We're old. These things are new to us.

DAVID   It's not that. I just find it distressing that my parents have become such a cliché.

PHYLLIS   You were always good mechanically. Hilary Klein asked you over to fix her stereo when you were fourteen. She loved you. So did her mother.

DAVID   Yes, if I remember correctly, I had my way with both of them in the garage.

PHYLLIS   Her brother's very delicate-looking. You think he might be?

DAVID   I don't know, Ma. I'll check the newsletter.

PHYLLIS   Don't be such a smart-ass.

She crosses to the refrigerator and pours juice for David. He sits at the table.

PHYLLIS (*cont.*)   Listen, David, I want to talk to you about some things. Your father will be home soon; they usually play till three. We don't have much time.

DAVID   Mom, are you having an affair?

PHYLLIS   If I was, I wouldn't tell you.

DAVID   Ooh, listen to you.

PHYLLIS   David, I want you to stop taking money from your father.

DAVID   What? What are you talking about?

PHYLLIS   I know he gives you—I'm not stupid. Besides, we talk. Children think their parents never talk to each other.

DAVID It's not a lot.

PHYLLIS Enough is enough.

DAVID Mom, I'm embarking on an artistic career, it takes time before you can make enough to live decently. Especially now.

PHYLLIS He can't afford it. Money's tight. Your father's having problems.

DAVID Dad? What happened?

PHYLLIS Some bad investments. Everybody's dying.

DAVID What about at Pearson? They're indestructible, I thought.

PHYLLIS Nobody's paying their credit card bills. People are running up their cards and not paying. They declare bankruptcy or just let the numbers skyrocket. They don't care anymore. They think, Screw the system. And then there are people like you . . .

DAVID People like me?

PHYLLIS Your age, dying. They spend like crazy and then die, they don't care.

DAVID Good for them.

PHYLLIS Maybe so, but it's not good for your father. Pearson goes after the families, but that takes time, and there's usually nothing there.

DAVID Goddamn.

PHYLLIS Look, your father would never admit any of this to you, so I want you to do this for me. If he offers you anything, you refuse. Find something else. All right?

DAVID All right.

PHYLLIS After all, you're old enough now . . .

DAVID All right.

PHYLLIS You are spoiled, David, you know that.

DAVID I said "all right," didn't I?

PHYLLIS Fine.

DAVID I've been talking to a friend at NYU about doing some teaching in the musical theater program. I'll discuss the similarities of scenic elements in works by Verdi and Jerry Herman. I like to lecture people.

PHYLLIS Good. Thank you, sweetheart. You're a good boy, you really are.

DAVID What about Suzanne?

PHYLLIS What?

DAVID I know he gives her too. We talk. Parents think their children never talk to each other.

PHYLLIS She'll have to cut back.

DAVID But with the baby on the way?

Phyllis stands at the sink, her back turned.

DAVID (*cont.*) Mom, what? Is there a problem with the baby? Mom?

PHYLLIS There's a problem.

DAVID Oh, God, no. Did she miscarry? Nobody's told me anything.

PHYLLIS I'm not supposed to say. Suzanne would kill me.

DAVID It's a little late for that now.

PHYLLIS Please, David, leave it alone.

DAVID Mom, I'll call her right now if you don't tell me.

PHYLLIS She may not keep it.

DAVID Why not?

PHYLLIS They did that test at Oxy. Rob took her in.

DAVID And?

PHYLLIS It's gonna be like you.

Pause.

DAVID They can tell that?

PHYLLIS So it seems. I had to tell you, David. That's why I called. I know how to use the cable, I'm not a moron.

DAVID Are they sure?

PHYLLIS They're doctors. They never say they're sure, they just tell you enough to destroy you.

DAVID And you really think she's going to . . . No, Suzanne would never even think of doing that.

PHYLLIS Don't be so sure.

DAVID What did she say to you?

PHYLLIS She goes back and forth. You know your sister. As of this morning, she doesn't want it.

DAVID I can't believe this. Well, what can we do? Do you want me to talk to her?

PHYLLIS Maybe, I don't know. I'm confused. I wanted your perspective. You always see things a different way, I thought it would help.

165

DAVID   You want me to stop her from getting rid of it?

PHYLLIS   No. Absolutely not. It's her decision. It's the woman's choice.

DAVID   Then what?

PHYLLIS   I don't know.

DAVID   Ma, you knew I'd be upset. Why did you bring me into this?

PHYLLIS   I just . . . I kept thinking of Gloria Myers. My friend.

DAVID   With the dying mother? I don't understand.

PHYLLIS   All these years, I've been telling myself we just lost touch or that we grew apart. But that wasn't it. I dropped her. I pushed her out of my life. I was afraid she'd become sick and I'd have to go through it with her. I would have to help take care of her. I didn't think I was strong enough. Or I didn't think it was worth it. She was my best friend. We went to dances together, studied for the college boards. I loved her, never had another girlfriend like her, to this day—not in this neighborhood. Yesterday, I decided to look her up. I figured, maybe it's not too late.

DAVID   And?

PHYLLIS   She moved away years ago.

DAVID   And? Did you speak to her?

PHYLLIS   She's dead. Fifteen years already. Killed herself. With pills. She was getting sick and she didn't want to be a burden to anyone.

DAVID   I'm sorry, Mom.

PHYLLIS   There were twenty years in between. Twenty years when I could have had a best friend and I didn't. Because

I'm weak. Because I didn't love her enough. I have to live with that. Now I'm afraid Suzanne could make the same mistake and never know it.

DAVID Then tell her.

PHYLLIS I can't. I have to be supportive.

DAVID Well, I don't.

PHYLLIS David, please. This is her child. And Rob's.

DAVID I don't see why this is even an issue.

PHYLLIS That's because you're in the arts. To other people, it's a big deal.

DAVID Mom, I'm living it, and I don't see the problem. What difference does it make?

PHYLLIS Come on, wouldn't you rather be . . . ?

DAVID No. Maybe I did once, but not anymore. I have a happy life. I'm in a community. Are you?

PHYLLIS David, I read the obits every week.

DAVID And everybody's dying.

PHYLLIS But wouldn't you rather . . . ?

DAVID Mom, please. That's like asking wouldn't blacks rather be white?

PHYLLIS Well, wouldn't they? David, it's common sense.

DAVID Only because they spend their lives being shit on for what isn't their fault.

PHYLLIS That doesn't change the reality. In this society, anyone would rather . . .

DAVID Be you.

PHYLLIS (*Stung*)   Don't be cruel, David. You know what I'm saying.

DAVID   Fine. This is ridiculous. Look, the question is hypothetical.

PHYLLIS   Not anymore. The hypothalamus is in question. Or whatever it is. I still don't understand what they're saying.

DAVID   That it's biological, it's all natural. Congratulations, Ma, you're finally off the hook.

PHYLLIS   Mmm, right. I don't buy that. It's gotta be my fault. I must have dressed you funny. Or, I don't know, if only I hadn't taken your temperature that way.

Pause.

DAVID   Mom, what would you have done? I have to know.

PHYLLIS   David, we love you.

DAVID   But if you had known.

PHYLLIS   It was a different time. Different attitudes.

DAVID   Not so different.

PHYLLIS   You were always a joy. The delivery was a breeze, you came out singing and dancing. (*Singing.*)   "Matchmaker, matchmaker, make me a . . ."

Their eyes meet.

DAVID   Now I understand. That's why you can't talk to her yourself. Of course. Because you would have done the same thing. You would have killed me.

PHYLLIS David, you stop that. You are my son. I raised you. I wiped your tush. I held your head over the toilet when you were sick. I gave my life for you and your sister.

DAVID Then tell Suzanne to keep the baby.

PHYLLIS I can't.

DAVID You have to. Mom, don't you see what this means? For all of us.

PHYLLIS I can't tell her anything. How can I? She's seen what I've been through with you.

DAVID What have you been through?

PHYLLIS I've seen my child become something . . . different. That hurts, David. If you were a parent, you'd understand. This isn't what I wanted for you.

DAVID Well, get over it!

PHYLLIS It's not that easy. I can't.

DAVID You could. But you don't want to. So you're letting her kill me.

PHYLLIS No, David, no.

DAVID You're killing me.

PHYLLIS No, don't say that.

WALTER (*From offstage*) Phyllis? (*He enters, casually dressed.*) Hey, look who's here, the Wunderkind. Hey, kiddo.

DAVID Hi, Dad.

WALTER (*Kisses Phyllis's cheek and pours a cup of coffee*) I played pretty good today. Took Dennis Kaplan in straight sets. You should've heard him. Wouldn't shut up about

Denise's wedding. Like I want to hear about his buck-toothed kids. Everyone knows we've got the best kids in this neighborhood. The smartest, the best-looking.

DAVID   Mom told me about Suzanne.

WALTER   (*To Phyllis*)   I thought she told you not to say anything.

PHYLLIS   It wasn't right, Walter. I had to. He had to know.

WALTER   So. Look, it's their decision, David. If you get married and start a family it will be your decision. We're liberal people, maybe too much so. We let each of our children live their own lives.

DAVID   What would you have done?

WALTER   What?

PHYLLIS   He wants to know if we had known . . .

WALTER   What nonsense. We didn't. We didn't know.

PHYLLIS   I told him it was a different time.

WALTER   That it was.

DAVID   I don't think the date has anything to do with it. Nothing much has changed.

WALTER   Well, maybe you're right. Phyllis, you have any of that cheese?

DAVID   Goddamn it. Why is it so hard for you people to answer?

WALTER   Because we don't want to. David, I gotta tell you, for a smart kid, you're pretty stupid.

PHYLLIS   Walter, please.

DAVID   Why don't you want to? What are you hiding?

WALTER   Why do you want to do this? Huh, David? What good is it gonna do?

DAVID   I think I have a right to know.

WALTER   A right? You've got some nerve. "A right." We've given you everything a kid could ask for your whole life. You have no more rights.

PHYLLIS   This is silly. Boys, you're fighting over nothing.

DAVID   No, we're not.

WALTER   You're upset because you don't know what I feel inside? Well, tough. I don't even know what I feel inside.

DAVID (*Crosses angrily to the door*)   Bullshit, Dad. You know. You just don't have the guts to tell me.

WALTER   That's it. Okay. You got it.

PHYLLIS   Walter, don't.

WALTER   No, if he wants to be so dramatic and make a scene to find out "the truth," whatever that is, then fine.

DAVID   I do.

Flames from the "Magic Fire" flicker and rise in the sky behind the scene.

WALTER   All right. The answer is, "Who knows?" Maybe you'd be here, maybe you wouldn't. Maybe Suzanne would be an only child. Maybe we wouldn't have to think about the things you make us think about. If you want to know what I really feel, I'll tell you. I think you're sick and diseased and if there were a cure, I'd want you cured. That's how I feel. And even though your mother may refuse to admit it, deep down, she feels the same way.

PHYLLIS   Don't you speak for me.

WALTER   Fine. Now, you can tell us till you're blue in the face that it's irrational and we're narrow-minded but it won't make any difference. That's just the way it is. Still, it doesn't change anything. You're our only son and we love you. We love you very much, David, always have and always will. There's your answer.

The flames disappear. A short pause.

DAVID   Thank you. I appreciate your honesty. It's refreshing.

PHYLLIS   Don't listen to him, David. He doesn't mean it.

WALTER   Will you stop it, Phyllis. He can handle it. He's a man now. He's tough.

DAVID   Getting tougher by the minute.

WALTER   Good. Atta boy. That's right. You look good. Doesn't he look good? So, when are you going to come play tennis with me?

DAVID   Dad, you're a demon on the court. I wouldn't have a chance.

WALTER   Aah. Hey, mister, you need any money to tide you over? (*He takes money out of his wallet and offers it.*)

DAVID   No, that's okay.

PHYLLIS   Don't spoil him, Walter.

WALTER   What spoil, he works hard. Here. Take, take.

DAVID   No, that's all right, Dad. I don't need it. I'm starting to do some teaching on the side at NYU. Next week. It pays well.

WALTER   That's terrific.

172

DAVID Yeah. I have to go.

PHYLLIS David, you want any food to take home?

DAVID No. Thanks, Mom. (*He takes a long look at both of them.*) Thanks. Bye. (*He exits. A slight pause.*)

WALTER That's good about NYU.

PHYLLIS Mmm. Yeah. (*She looks at him.*)

WALTER Don't look.

He exits right. Phyllis is left alone. She takes a moment to regain her composure.

SCENE TWO

Phyllis addresses the audience:

PHYLLIS We live in the Information Age. It's true. Every
Sunday, while Walter plays tennis, I sit in bed with all *The
New York Times* from the week, Monday to Sunday. The kids
make fun of me. They say, "Mom, read The Week In
Review, that's all you need. You're gonna be out of date
anyway." Still, I lie there reading everything I didn't get to.
It's a compulsion, a disease. I'm so afraid I'll be caught in
conversation without knowing what Anthony Lewis wrote
about Israel on Tuesday and I'll be sent to Jewish-liberal
detention. I get very nervous. Anyway, it takes me the whole
day and I usually finish the week's pile just in time for *60
Minutes* which we watch to see if Mike Wallace is destroying
anyone we know. That's how I start the week. My brain is so
full of news and issues, opinions and statistics, that sometimes
I have to read Danielle Steele just to clear my head.
Otherwise, I wake up screaming, "I'll take social injustice for
six hundred, Alex!" You always hear people say we don't

173

know enough. We're all ignorant, that's why the country's falling apart. Well, I don't see that, not for a minute. If you ask me, I think we all know too damn much. We're all being oppressed by information that has nothing to do with our experience. All we can do is react. Years ago, we didn't know about blacks. Not really. They were blacks, live and let live. We didn't know about sex, how it was supposed to feel, what to do. Who thought it was supposed to be any better than it was? We didn't know about addictions, about life in prison, about the plight of transexual, cross-dressing priests. Right? Years ago, you lived your life. Now, we have to seem so concerned all the time about every terrible, unfair thing that goes on, that we all walk around with these pained Barbara Walters expressions plastered on our faces. And what good is it doing? Not only have we completely failed at helping anybody else, but we have taken the beauty and simplicity out of our own lives. Am I right? (*Pause.*) This is a terrible thing I'm saying. I know. It sounds like I'm advocating ignorance, wanting to look the other way. But I'm not. I think people are good and should be left alone. If they could just do what their hearts tell them to do, everything would be all right. If they would just listen to their hearts. Sometimes, I hear people around here say, "If my daughter did this," or "If my son was like that, I'd run him out of the house." And I want to say, "No, you wouldn't. That's very easy for you to say, sitting there with your Vuitton bag, driving your Infiniti, and expecting the world to cater to you. But you don't know how you'd feel. You don't know how your heart breaks when the world around you doesn't match your expectations. You have no idea." That's what I want to tell them. But it's none of their business. So I don't say anything. I just sit there. I don't say anything.

Music: The "Fate Motive" from Die Walküre. *Phyllis's kitchen moves offstage as the lights come up on Suzanne and Rob's apartment. There is a knock at the door. Suzanne enters nervously from the kitchen. She looks at the door, not knowing what to do. The knocking continues. Finally, she speaks.*

SUZANNE Yes?

DAVID (*Through the door*) Open up, you rich bitch.

SUZANNE David, you shit.

DAVID (*Opens the door with his key*) I'm gonna smash your Krups cappuccino maker.

SUZANNE Very funny.

DAVID Hi, Sis. I called Bloomingdale's, they said you left early, so I thought I'd catch you, see how you're doing.

SUZANNE I had a headache.

DAVID That reminds me, this is for you. (*He takes out a CD from his pocket.*)

SUZANNE *Gypsy.* Well, at least it's not opera.

DAVID This is the Angela Lansbury recording. I already gave you the original with Merman, but I saw last time I was here that you still haven't opened it. So I figure two different versions improves my chances.

SUZANNE You're really starting to piss me off.

DAVID Please, if I wanted to piss you off, I'd bring Tyne Daly.

SUZANNE Put it with the others. I know how you like them in alphabetical order.

DAVID My pleasure.

SUZANNE I'm making dinner. There's not enough food, you can't stay.

She exits to the kitchen. David looks at the CD collection. He picks up a boxed opera set.

DAVID I don't believe it! It can't be! "Vittoria!"

SUZANNE What are you yelling about?

DAVID The *La Bohéme* is out of the plastic. There's hope!

SUZANNE (*From the kitchen*) Don't get excited. *Moonstruck* was on cable.

DAVID From me it's boring . . .

SUZANNE Honestly, David, I wish you'd stop bringing us that stuff. It puts me in a very awkward position.

DAVID I don't take it personally. Besides, it's not for you anymore.

SUZANNE Rob has no interest.

DAVID Somebody will.

Pause. Suzanne enters.

SUZANNE Mom told you. I knew she would. This family talks too much.

DAVID So then it's true. How can you? Do you realize what you're doing?

SUZANNE Funny, I don't remember asking for your input.

DAVID Suzanne, I can't just sit by and let this happen.

SUZANNE Stop it, David. Stop it before you say another word. You have no right to come in here and tell me what to do. Especially after Marnie Eisner.

DAVID What? Marnie Eisner? I can't believe you're throwing that in my face.

SUZANNE You were a junior in high school. You came to me in a panic, your voice was cracking. You said, "Suzanne, I don't know what to do. I can't have a kid. I won't be able to go to college." Remember?

DAVID It just happened.

SUZANNE Do you remember how I went with you to the bank and we got out some of your bar mitzvah money? Do you?

DAVID Of course I do. I remember.

SUZANNE I brought the two of you to that clinic that smelled like Windex. I held her hand. I held your hand. I took care of both of you and we got it done.

DAVID Yes, you were wonderful.

SUZANNE You were so afraid Mom and Dad would find out.

DAVID Now it's what they pray for.

SUZANNE Whatever happened to Marnie?

DAVID She lives with a woman in Seattle. I think we both knew something wasn't right. So, what's your point?

SUZANNE I supported you. No questions asked. Now I want you to do the same thing.

DAVID I'm sorry, I can't do that.

SUZANNE David!

DAVID It's not the same thing. Not even remotely. Marnie got pregnant by accident. Her life would have been badly damaged, as would mine, and so would the kid's. You and

Rob wanted this baby. You can afford it. You're ready to be parents. But now, because you know something about this person you've created that you don't care for, you're ending his life.

SUZANNE It's my choice, David. It's my right to choose. And stop saying "his."

DAVID Ah, yes, the right of choice—the last refuge of the morally indefensible. We demand the right of choice when we know deep down what we want to do is wrong. Necessary maybe, regrettable yes, but definitely wrong. We demand our God-given right to take the easy way out.

SUZANNE You don't believe that.

DAVID Yes. Right now, I think I do.

SUZANNE No, I know you don't. You're talking like some right-wing fundamentalist crackpot. Coming here in your own little "Operation Rescue." Don't you dare give me a sermon as if you had morality on your side. I think we know you don't.

DAVID That's not what this is about. I would never take away your right. I'd march in the streets and write my congressman to make sure you keep it. But this is something new. This is a decision that no one's ever had to make before. I'm asking you to choose carefully. Please. Think it over.

SUZANNE I have.

DAVID Think harder. How can you do this to me?

SUZANNE Oh, this is about you, is it?

DAVID You're erasing me from the world. You're rubbing me out. Why? I thought you loved me.

SUZANNE Don't play those games with me. They won't work.

Beat.

DAVID What does Rob say?

SUZANNE Rob says a lot. He says he'll be patient and support me in my choice but I should hurry up and decide. And if I feel up to the challenge of raising this one, then he is too. The message is coming through loud and clear: Why put ourselves through this? And, frankly, I don't blame him. This baby was going to change our lives and make everything better. Not that things are bad, but, I don't know, we could use a clear sense of purpose. Now the whole thing is tainted. I wish we didn't know, but we do. And it's a problem.

DAVID What wouldn't be a problem with you?

SUZANNE Oh, please.

DAVID What if you found out the kid was going to be ugly, or smell bad, or have an annoying laugh, or need really thick glasses?

SUZANNE Come on, David. We're talking about something pretty serious.

DAVID But where do we stop? You know we have relatives who died for less. So now we have this technology, what are we going to do with it? It starts with us, Suzanne.

SUZANNE Oh, shut up! Shut up! Shut up! I can't take it anymore.

DAVID That's because you know I'm right.

SUZANNE No, it's because I'm sick of you. I'm tired of your lectures and the way you talk down to all of us. Goddamn it, I am so sick of being "the shallow one." Everybody dotes

179

on you, with all your deep feelings and higher interests. The truth is you're just a spoiled brat who always has to have his own way.

DAVID (*Crossing to the door*)   Yes. You're right. And so is Stephen. I'm a horrible little shit. I should get the hell out and grow up. And maybe I will. But when I'm done, I'll come back and say the same things and I'll still be right. (*He opens the door.*)

SUZANNE (*Faltering*)   Why are you doing this?

DAVID (*Stops in the doorway*)   Because I'm fighting for my life. Do you have any idea how horrifying this is? To find out that the people who brought you into this world wish that they had slammed the door?

SUZANNE   This family has been very good to you in every way, David. Don't play the martyr. We all love you, you know that. We love you.

DAVID   Then love him.

SUZANNE   I don't have the strength for it. I wish to God I was as strong as you are, but I'm not. I can't take it.

DAVID   Is that a good enough reason?

SUZANNE   Probably not. But, think of that little boy. What would it be like for him? You know how people are. How would Rob and I be able to help him, feeling the way we do? It wouldn't be fair to any of us. David, what kind of mother would I be if I didn't understand my child?

DAVID   I'd say you'd be pretty typical.

SUZANNE   I doubt that. This isn't typical. You're not typical. There's nothing typical about you. You're still a mystery to me.

180

DAVID Just like you are to me. But I consider that an asset.

SUZANNE David, I know it's been hard for you. When I think of all the times I've heard you say you're lonely or scared . . .

DAVID You never feel that way?

SUZANNE You tell me your problems and it terrifies me.

DAVID Don't make me regret sharing my life with you.

SUZANNE Why should we put someone else through that if we can help it? Why isn't it more humane to wait until we can bring a child with no disadvantages into the world?

DAVID Because we'll lose too much. Don't you see? All the things you love about me are tied to that one element that makes you queasy. Every human being is a tapestry. You pull one thread, one undesirable color, and the art unravels. You end up staring at the walls. When Brünnhilde dies . . .

SUZANNE Oh, God, here we go. I should have known this was coming.

DAVID When she throws herself into the fire and lets the gods die with her, she is hoping something better will rise out of the ashes. She doesn't stick around to choose what that something is. She leaves that to Nature and Fate. Hers is an act of love. That's our only hope.

SUZANNE That's beautiful. I can skip Course in Miracles this week. Are you finished?

DAVID One more story and then I'll go. You can battle it out with your own conscience when I'm gone. But I won't leave here until you hear about Siegmund and Sieglinde.

SUZANNE (*Sighs. She sits on the sofa and glances at her watch.*) Go ahead.

DAVID Siegmund and Sieglinde are brother and sister, twins, separated in childhood. Years later, they meet and they fall in love.

SUZANNE This is gross.

DAVID For once, will you open your ears and really listen?! This is the only way I can make sense of things.

SUZANNE (*Quietly*) Sorry.

DAVID They fall in love. And then they realize who they are. But this knowledge only spurs them on further, and in a fit of ecstasy, they consummate their feelings for each other.

SUZANNE I don't know where you're going with this, but I think I better tell you, it's out of the question.

DAVID (*Sits next to her*) Siegmund is killed for his crime against the laws of morality. And Sieglinde, facing a life without her beloved brother, seeks only death. But before she ends her life, Brünnhilde tells her that she cannot die. For she is carrying Siegmund's child. She is bringing her brother's child into the world. Sieglinde is overjoyed. She hides in the forest and gives her life in the delivery of a new incarnation of her brother.

SUZANNE What happens to her son?

Music: the "Siegfried Idyll" played softly in the background.

DAVID He is Siegfried, the bravest hero the world has ever known. Without fear, he breaks all of the gods' outdated laws in two. He follows his heart and what he learns from Nature. He understands the calls of birds. He's beautiful.

The sky has turned clear and radiant.

SUZANNE And what does he do?

DAVID He slays a dragon and walks through rings of Magic Fire. He then awakens Brünnhilde from her sleep. She tells him that she is the feminine side of himself and the two proclaim their love. By joining with her, Siegfried reaches man's true potential, both masculine and feminine, brave and loving.

SUZANNE What happens to Siegfried?

Gradually, the sky grows dark and cloudy and the music fades out.

DAVID The world, which is cruel and corrupt, destroys him. He is stabbed in the back by evil men. Such a hero cannot survive in a decaying civilization.

SUZANNE So Sieglinde went through all that pain for nothing.

DAVID She brought a beautiful hero into the world.

SUZANNE And the world destroyed him. I don't want that to happen to my child.

DAVID Then change the world.

SUZANNE David, look at me. I couldn't finish pre-med, you want me to change the world.

DAVID You can do this.

SUZANNE David, you know I don't like to be tested. I just want the life Mom and Dad had when we were kids. I want to live in the world we saw growing up. That's all I ask.

DAVID We can't have that. Even if it existed in the first place, which I doubt, it's out of our grasp now. We don't have what our parents had. We don't have the faith, we don't have the money. We don't have the leaders, the confidence, or trust. And so, what do we do to combat the malaise? We shut ourselves off. We shrink from any challenge and take the easy way out. We've become lazy and fearful because we doubt our ability to love. Without question. I know you, Suzanne. You have the strength. You can do this. You're not shallow.

SUZANNE   You don't think so?

DAVID   No. That's a card you play because it's easy. But that's not you. I know you. There's greatness in you, Suzanne Gold. Don't be afraid. Awaken. Usher in a new era, take care of your child. Okay? Okay?

SUZANNE   (*After a moment*)   You know what I was just thinking about?

DAVID   No, what?

SUZANNE   Your bar mitzvah.

DAVID   Really?

SUZANNE   You wore that brown three-piece suit with Pierre Cardin's name written like fifty times on the back of the vest. And a really thick tie.

DAVID   You were wearing culottes.

SUZANNE   They were gauchos. But who's counting? I was so proud of you. I remember when you finished your Haftorah and you looked up, you looked right at me.

DAVID   You gave me one of these. (*He wipes his brow and makes a "whew" sound.*)

SUZANNE   I remember thinking, how incredible. I look in his face and I see my own.

DAVID   At the party, I danced the first slow dance with you.

SUZANNE   What was the song? It was some Top 40 ballad.

DAVID   It was Roberta Flack.

SUZANNE   Oh, God, you're right.

DAVID   (*Quietly sings the song "Killing Me Softly"*)   "I heard he sang a good song, I heard he had a style . . ."

David rises. He takes Suzanne's hand and leads her to the center of the room. She joins him in a very slow, almost motionless dance.

SUZANNE   Oh, God.

DAVID   (*Singing*)   "And so I came to see him to listen for a while."

SUZANNE   (*Singing*)   "And there he was this young boy, a stranger to my eyes."

BOTH   (*Singing softly and dancing*)   "Strumming my pain with his fingers, singing my life with his words . . ."

The song trails off. David hugs her.

DAVID   Don't. Please don't. Don't do it. Don't.

Music: The "Love Gaze" from Act I of Die Walküre. *Rob has appeared downstage left to watch his wife and brother-in-law dance. The lights fade and David and Suzanne exit.*

SCENE THREE

Rob examines the DNA model. He turns and addresses the audience:

ROB   My favorite toy as a kid was always Lego. I must have had more Lego blocks by the time I was ten than that city in Denmark where they have that whole Lego metropolis. I could never understand the attraction of a toy that came ready in the package. What good was that? I would beg my parents to only buy me toys that said "Assembly Required."

And then I would see how fast I could put the stuff together without ever reading the instructions. It didn't always come out looking like the picture on the box, but it was more important for me to attain that feeling of fulfillment. The power of the creator. I know it sounds ridiculous, but I think my road to a career in genetic research was paved with Lego. I always had a fascination with components; how things are put together, how to take them apart, how to change them. It still excites me. I sit there in the lab, surrounded by these million-dollar machines under those buzzing fluorescent lights and I think, Why not with people? There's obviously a lot, we can all agree, that needs to be corrected. Or can at least be improved. Just look at the amount of suffering, inward and outward, all around us. Let's use every weapon we have to combat it. Is that such a horrible thing to think? Of course not. Well, my father turned bright red when I said something similar at the dinner table. He called me a Nazi. "You are hateful," he said. "Why has God punished us with a Nazi for a son?" So then I called him a backward little man living in the Stone Age. At which point, my mother started crying and running around lighting candles. Things haven't been the same since. (*Beat.*) I had pretty much put that whole argument out of my mind until David started his crusade. It's a complicated issue, of course it is. I don't deny that. But I can make a helluva case that what Oxy does is a lot more useful and productive for society than spending tax dollars to have fat Germans walk around a stage with helmets and spears for five hours. How dare he raise the specter of genocide, like some college kid saying anything to win an argument! The nerve of him. Suzanne and I have enough problems without him poking around her conscience. Or mine.

Let's face it, do I want a kid who's going to know every time he looks in Suzanne's eyes that he's not the one she wanted? I know what that's like. My wife is not someone who has learned to live with disappointment. And I have much too well. Someone has to tell her that. (*Pause.*)   The bottom line is this: Look around you. You think it's so easy to have a family today? The family is an endangered species. There are kids on the streets, broken homes, abuse. Why stack the deck against us? Why walk into a no-win situation? Don't believe what David says. This isn't an opera about the fate of humanity.

Walter and Phyllis enter quietly through the front door. Walter puts down their coats and the two sit together on the sofa.

ROB (*cont.*)   It's the simple story of one family making a very private decision. He, of all people, should know to respect other people's privacy. We need to do what's right for us. Don't put the fate of the world on our shoulders. We can't carry the load.

Lights up in the apartment. The sky is bleak and colorless.

PHYLLIS   Is she all right?

ROB   She's still weak. But she's glad to be home.

PHYLLIS   Should I go in?

ROB   Just leave her alone. She'll be okay.

WALTER   Let her rest.

Pause.

PHYLLIS   So what did he say, Doctor—what is it—Hagen? (*Pronounced "Hay-gen"*)

WALTER   Phyllis.

PHYLLIS I want to hear it. We hardly hear from you in weeks, you cancel dinner, and now this. I want to know what happened. What did he say?

ROB Nothing. That there were complications.

PHYLLIS Tell me.

WALTER What good will it do?

PHYLLIS I want to know.

ROB There's always a danger when it's done after the fifth month. Dr. Hagen said there was a perforation during the procedure and Suzanne started hemorrhaging.

PHYLLIS She always bled badly as a little girl. Like me with a paper cut.

ROB It's genetic. Things got bad. He had to perform a hysterectomy.

PHYLLIS Oh, God.

WALTER Is there anything we can . . . ?

ROB Nothing. She never will.

PHYLLIS It's like a bad dream. Huh, Walter? It's a nightmare. When does it end? How many times do you have to have your heart broken? Huh, Walter?

WALTER I know. I know.

Pause.

PHYLLIS How are you doing, Rob?

ROB I'm all right.

PHYLLIS Have you spoken to your parents?

ROB No. Are you kidding?

PHYLLIS Did David call?

ROB I spoke to him last night. He hasn't called today.

WALTER That's surprising.

PHYLLIS He should be here.

ROB Why? He's done enough damage.

WALTER What's that supposed to mean?

ROB It's his fault. Christ, she was all set, she had made up her mind. We agreed. And then he had to interfere. He made us think too much.

PHYLLIS You can understand how he felt. It's a very personal issue to him.

ROB It was none of his business. You shouldn't have told him.

WALTER Maybe not.

PHYLLIS He's family. I had to tell him. I had to. I thought he would add a different perspective.

ROB We didn't need it. God, what is wrong with you people? Don't you have lives of your own? When are you going to leave your children alone? Stop calling, stop taking us to dinner and choosing the restaurant. Once, just once, I want to go where *I* want to go. All this closeness is suffocating.

WALTER Fine, you want us to leave you alone, fine.

PHYLLIS Rob, you're upset, it's understandable. Something terrible has happened.

ROB It's more than that. You know the first thing Suzanne said to me when it was over? "Did you call my parents?"

189

We had just lost any hope of having children and she's running to you to make her feel better. I don't know why I'm even here.

PHYLLIS   What are you saying? You're walking out? Is that what you're saying? Your wife needs you.

ROB   No, she needs you.

PHYLLIS   Don't you dare, Rob. Don't you dare.

WALTER   If he wants to go, let him go. She'll be all right. We can take care of her.

ROB   I know you can. You always do.

PHYLLIS   Walter, stop. Don't talk like that. I can't stand it.

WALTER   It's typical of their generation. They expect too much and then they cry bloody murder when things don't work out the way they want.

PHYLLIS   I'm dying from all this. I'm dying.

Suzanne appears upstage wearing a bathrobe.

WALTER   What are you doing up?

ROB   (*Goes to Suzanne*)   Are you okay? Take it easy. I'm here. I'm not going anywhere.

SUZANNE   I want to sit for a while.

ROB   (*Guides her slowly to a chair*)   Careful.

Suzanne sits. Rob stands by her.

SUZANNE   I figure you're all talking about me anyway.

PHYLLIS   It will be all right, sweetheart.

SUZANNE   No it won't.

WALTER Hey. Don't worry, Suzy Q. It's not the end of the world.

SUZANNE (*Dryly*) Oh, that's good.

PHYLLIS Sweetheart, tell us what happened.

WALTER Phyllis, she doesn't feel well.

SUZANNE No, it's all right. Might as well get it over with. What do you want to know?

PHYLLIS When did you change your mind?

ROB Which time?

WALTER What the hell is wrong with you?

Phyllis steps between Walter and Rob. Walter turns away. Phyllis sits.

SUZANNE It's okay, Dad, leave him alone. I was just about ready to have it done. I was. I was fine with it. But then David made his case. Oh, he's good. He should have been a lawyer. He made me feel like this Anita Bryant Nazi snuffing out my own brother in cold blood.

PHYLLIS Well, he shouldn't have done that. That wasn't right.

SUZANNE No, it wasn't. It was very easy for him. David could make his argument, make me cry, and leave. He wouldn't have to raise it. We would. The whole thing had a lot more to do with Rob and me than it did with David.

WALTER But you listened to him.

SUZANNE I couldn't help it. You know how he gets. I love David. I couldn't do that to him. So, I decided that I would handle it.

191

ROB We talked it over.

SUZANNE Rob was really good about it.

WALTER Very nice.

PHYLLIS You told me. I was happy. So, then what?

SUZANNE Then I started to show. Every morning, I would see it in the mirror and I'd start thinking these awful things. Mean, stupid things. I knew they were stupid. But I can't help what I think, can I? A person has no control over their feelings, right? That's what I told myself.

ROB She was wavering, I could tell. She kept wearing big sweaters so people wouldn't notice. So she didn't have to talk about it.

SUZANNE I got really upset, like maybe this was just too much for me.

PHYLLIS Suzanne, why didn't you come to me?

SUZANNE Why? Because you would have told David, that's why.

PHYLLIS No, I wouldn't. Not if you told me not to . . .

SUZANNE (*Turns away*) About a month ago, Rob asked Dr. Lodge to recommend a counselor, someone to help us prepare for what we were facing.

ROB Which was tricky because nobody's supposed to know about this. But Adrian found us someone he trusted.

WALTER You were going to a counselor?

PHYLLIS I couldn't talk about that type of thing with anyone.

192

SUZANNE   What a coincidence. Neither could I. We were in the cab on the way to our first appointment and I started freaking out.

ROB   I'd never seen her get like that. She started hyperventilating and wringing her hands.

SUZANNE   It was like the SAT's. I couldn't go through with it. I just couldn't. I wasn't prepared. I had to get it out.

WALTER   So you should have done it. Right then. Right away.

SUZANNE   We tried.

ROB   It took us over three weeks to find somebody willing to do it that late without asking why. Remember we couldn't tell anybody the reason.

SUZANNE   So much for freedom of choice.

ROB   Dr. Lodge refused to help. Didn't want the responsibility, he said. We found Hagen, we thought, just in time.

WALTER   That witch doctor. I should kill him.

SUZANNE   It's funny. I knew there was a risk of things going wrong, so I was sure it wouldn't happen because things never happen when you expect them. Wrong again. And now it's all over.

ROB   Stop it, Suzanne. It's not your fault.

SUZANNE   Then whose is it?

PHYLLIS   It's mine. I should have known. I should have stopped you.

SUZANNE   Mom, would you please not co-opt my failure? I'd like to have my own trauma for a change. We can cut the "sins of the mother" routine, I'm tired of it. I did this. It was time for me to take responsibility for my life. (*Laughing sadly to herself.*) Look how good I did.

The phone rings. Rob answers.

ROB Hello? Oh, hi. (*To the others.*) It's Stephen.

WALTER What's he doing, calling here?

PHYLLIS Where's David? He should be here. Tell him I want to see him. (*Calling into the phone.*) David, you should be here!

ROB (*Into phone*) She's doing okay. I brought her home this morning. Yeah. What? Uh-huh. (*He goes to the CD collection.*) Okay, I see it. Yeah. Okay, bye.

WALTER Is David coming?

ROB No. He asked Stephen to call, to make sure Suzanne was all right. He told me to look for a note.

WALTER What?

Rob pulls a note out of the boxed Ring Cycle.

PHYLLIS How did he get it here?

SUZANNE David has a key.

PHYLLIS But why would he stick it in there?

SUZANNE It's a place we'd never look.

Rob unfolds the note and finds David's keys to the apartment. He hands them to Suzanne. He sits on the floor next to her.

WALTER What's it say? Read it.

ROB "To the last of the Golds: I want to express my deepest sympathy for what has happened. And so does Stephen.

This is a difficult time, I know, and I am sorry that I am not there with you, but I'm afraid I can never see any of you again. I never . . ."

WALTER   What?

SUZANNE   Let him finish.

The sky turns red.

ROB   "I never dreamed I would or could leave you all, but now I know that I have no choice. You are creating a new world for yourselves and it is one of which I will never be a part. Please, however, don't pity me, for I am not alone."

WALTER   He's so dramatic.

PHYLLIS   Oh my God.

The sky returns slowly to a peaceful blue.

ROB   "I know you love me. And I love you all so much. But we are weak people. You don't love me enough to allow me into your family, and I don't love you enough not to notice. Don't try to contact me, I won't respond. This is the dawn of a new era. *Ruhe, ruhe, du Gott.* Love, David."

Pause.

PHYLLIS   Do something, Walter, call him.

WALTER   He told us not to.

PHYLLIS   Suzanne, he'll listen to you. Call him. Say you're sorry.

SUZANNE   No. He's right.

PHYLLIS   What?

SUZANNE   He's right.

PHYLLIS What are you saying?

WALTER It's what he wants.

PHYLLIS Oh, God. Oh, my God.

WALTER Let him go, Phyllis. Just let him go.

PHYLLIS No! I won't let him go. He's our son. I can't let him go! We're not the people who cut off their children. We're not the people who do that. Walter, please!

WALTER *Shh*. Phyllis, *shh*.

ROB Sit down, Mom.

SUZANNE (*Flatly, remembering David's story*) "Rest. Rest."

Pause. There is a knock at the door. The lights fade as the apartment walls return and re-form the apartment as it appeared in the opening moments of the play. Music: Prelude to Siegfried, *Act Two.*

David enters downstage. The music fades out.

DAVID A few weeks later, Stephen and I celebrated our third anniversary. To prove to him how much I had matured in my new sense of independence and manhood, I let him arrange the evening. He took me to a Bruce Springsteen concert. And people say *Tristan* is long! But I liked it. I'm used to hearing people sing for four hours without understanding a word. Afterwards, we went home and gave each other gifts. We're not crazy about crystal and glass, so we checked out what the third anniversary is according to tradition. Anyone know? Leather. That we liked. (*He smiles.*) Relax. He gave me a wallet. (*He looks at the family, still in tableau.*) I've been true to my word. To this day, I haven't spoken to the Golds. It hasn't been easy. More than once my mother showed up at our apartment in the middle of the night, crying and pounding on the door. But I just buried my head in Stephen's chest until my father came and dragged her away. Dad didn't share Mom's flair for melodrama. He just sent me checks, which he knew I wouldn't cash, accompanied by notes that read, "How can you do this to your mother?" I never heard from Suzanne. She understood. But maybe they all do now. I never hear from anyone anymore.

(*Beat.*)   Once, just once, I almost broke down and called the Golds. A conductor friend of mine invited Stephen and me over for dinner to introduce us to his very distinguished new boyfriend. None other than Dr. Adrian Lodge. "Jewish anti-Semites, they're the worst." Right, Ma? (*He smiles.*)   I hardly ever listen to *The Ring Cycle* now. Still, I talk about it in my course at NYU. I'm famous for my lecture about the Magic Fire, not because it's so insightful, but because I usually break down and cry. (*He lectures.*)   So, what is the Magic Fire? Shaw wrote, It is the Lie that must hide the Truth. It's the teachings of the Church, the laws of the State. It's the fire of Hell that will burn you if you question what you're told. It's everything you're afraid of because you're supposed to be. But then how come Siegfried walks right through it without so much as singeing an eyebrow? It's not because he's such a hero. Most of the time he's played by a tenor who looks like Mussolini in a blond wig. It's because the Magic Fire is a fraud.

Music: The statement of the "Love and Redemption" theme that ends The Ring.

DAVID (*cont.*)   It can't hurt you. Mankind will keep creating new and better worlds, and there will always be those who are left, for whatever reason, on the other side of the Magic Fire. If only we were brave enough to walk through that fire, and unlock that door, we would awaken another part

197

of our soul. And we would know what it means to truly love. Without question. (*The music swells.*) Just listen to that.

The glorious final chord hovers, suspended over David as he takes a seat downstage and looks at the Golds, still in tableau. The last thread of sound dies away as the lights slowly fade to black.

Curtain.

END OF PLAY

IF MEMORY SERVES

This play is dedicated to
Gary Morris
and to the memory of
Esther Sherman

If Memory Serves was presented by Charles H. Duggan, Ostar Enterprises, and Jennifer Manocherian, in association with Richard Frankel and Marc Routh, at the Promenade Theater, New York City, on December 12, 1999, with the following cast:

LINDA SIMMONS, HELEN MENKEN	Marilyn Sokol
DIANE BARROW	Elizabeth Ashley
PAM GOLDMAN	Melanie Vesey
RUSSELL BURKE, ADAM BURKE	Sam Trammell
PAUL MICHAEL	Jeff Whitty
TAYLOR MCDONALD	Ron Mathews
DR. MARGARET THURM, MRS. KENNEDY	Lynda Gravátt
STAN BURKE	Tony Campisi
Director	Leonard Foglia
Scenic Design	Michael McGarty
Costume Design	Ilona Somogyi
Lighting Design	Russell H. Champa
Sound Design	Laura Grace Brown
Original Music	Peter Matz
Casting	Bruce H. Newberg and James Calleri
Production Stage Manager	Patrick Ballard
Stage Manager	Linda Barnes

The world premiere of *If Memory Serves* was presented at The Pasadena Playhouse in California (Lars Hansen, executive director, and Sheldon Epps, artistic director,) by special arrangement with Charles H. Duggan on September 20, 1998, with the following cast:

LINDA SIMMONS, HELEN MENKEN	Marilyn Sokol
DIANE BARROW	Brooke Adams
PAM GOLDMAN, MICHELLE★	Pamela Segall Adlon
RUSSELL BURKE, ADAM BURKE	Michael Landes
PAUL MICHAEL	Bill Brochtrup
TAYLOR MCDONALD, TIM★	Steven Culp
DR. MARGARET THURM, MRS. KENNEDY	Paula Kelly
STAN BURKE, MR. WILCOX ★	David Groh

★The characters Michelle, Tim, and Mr. Wilcox were cut from the New York production.

Director	Leonard Foglia
Scenic Design	Michael McGarty
Lighting Design	Russell H. Champa
Costume Design	Chrisi Karvonides-Dushenko
Sound Design	Jon Gottlieb
Original Music	Peter Matz
Casting	Bruce H. Newberg
Production Stage Manager	Artie Gaffin
Stage Manager	Elizabeth Kingl

"Nothing that actually occurs is of the smallest importance."

—Oscar Wilde

ACT I

At Rise: the Oak Room at the Plaza Hotel in New York City.
LINDA SIMMONS, a daily gossip columnist, waits at a table,
sipping a martini. After a short musical "sting," she faces the
audience to speak her column.

LINDA   Monday column. We gossip peddlers often find
ourselves sitting alone in a restaurant, bar, or hotel lobby,
waiting patiently for a celebrity to join us. (God forbid they
should ever show up on time.)   At such moments, I usually
sit in the corner, sipping my martini, watching strangers
turn surreptitiously to look my way. I know it isn't me
they're staring at, they just want to know who's waiting in
the wings. It's like being a supporting character in the
opening scene of a play—setting the tone while everyone
waits for the star to make her entrance, to bring up the
lights and get things started. It's as if nothing really happens
until it happens with one of them. That's a lot of
responsibility. No wonder so many of them fall apart. Still,
it must feel fabulous to walk in and light up a room. How
do they do it?

The lights come up full as . . .

DIANE   I'm here, I didn't forget, I swear!

LINDA   Diane!

DIANE BARROW, *a beautiful woman of indeterminate age,*
enters. She is a star, well preserved, smartly dressed, radiant.

DIANE   We said six o'clock and I know I'm late.

LINDA Twenty minutes.

DIANE That's no excuse. And neither is the idiot in Pete's office whose fault it is. Oh, Linda, it is so good to see you! I can't remember the last time we had a chance to sit down and really talk.

LINDA Six years ago. The Golden Globes.

DIANE No. No, no, no. I refuse to believe that, I've missed you. I really have.

LINDA Likewise.

DIANE I think of you. And not just when I read your column, which I'm never in. You look fabulous, Linda, you never change.

LINDA Oh, please. I'm an old lady. But you! My God, Diane, looking at you, it's 1975.

DIANE Bite your tongue.

LINDA Why? That decade is coming back.

DIANE. Not if I can help it. Let's talk about *now*.

LINDA All right, sure. Do you mind if I tape this?

DIANE Oh, no, I prefer it.

LINDA Good. So do I.

DIANE You're the only journalist I respect, Linda, period. (*Linda moves the tape recorder closer to Diane.*) And you can print that if you like. I just spent fourteen hours being interviewed upstairs in my suite by reporters from all over the country and I had to bite my lip to keep from gagging.

LINDA Well, there's quite a range out there.

DIANE Idiots, all of them. I know, I'm sounding bitter and ungrateful but I can't help it. I've just been talking incessantly. Pete's done a great job putting me out there but sometimes I just want to scream. I just want to scream and run and hide away somewhere. Just to be myself for five lousy seconds. Just to . . . (*She trails off filled with emotion. Pause.*) I'm sorry.

LINDA Diane? We don't have to do this. If you'd like to call me later in the week . . .

DIANE Oh, no. You're a friend, Linda.

LINDA Yes. I am.

DIANE I can talk to you. You know me. You know what this trip means for me. Can you imagine? I'm promoting my "low-impact" workout video. Has it come to this?

LINDA Pete sent over the video. It's really very good.

DIANE Oh, it's fine, I know. And the career is not as terrible as all that. My assistant says I haven't bought a pet chimp yet, so I'm nowhere near rock bottom.

LINDA Of course not.

DIANE But life is just too damn long, isn't it? No one ever ends on a high.

LINDA Diane, you're depressing me.

DIANE Well, it's true. That's why everybody's so obsessed with Marilyn and James Dean, you know. Because they got out. They never had to live up to their early promise, did they? They never had to endure the crushing boredom of normal life.

LINDA Their lives ended in tragedy.

DIANE   And we love them for it. Please, God, save me from the uneventful life.

LINDA   You could hardly call your life uneventful. Your show was a classic. You were America's sweetheart. My God, Diane, you're an . . .

DIANE   If you say icon, I'll hit you. Pet peeve. It makes me feel like a yellow smiley face. Not a person. Not flesh and blood. You know, they run my show on that cable channel now. Every night.

LINDA   Yes, it's wonderful.

DIANE   It was damn good. The writing, the cast, everything. Maybe the best ever. Anyway, sometimes, I watch the reruns. I sit there in bed with cold cream on my face and watch myself twenty years ago. I can never remember what happens so I laugh at the jokes and follow the plot. And I'm telling you, I'm filled with such joy. There is so much warmth, so much intelligence and humor floating through that box. So much . . . youth. It makes me want to dance. And then a commercial will come on. And since I've been laughing and squinching my face up, I go into the bathroom to put on more moisturizer. And every time, I see myself in the mirror and it stops me cold. Who is that old lady with Lancôme Hydrative Lotion dripping from her chin? What on earth does she have to do with that radiant young woman on the screen? The answer is absolutely nothing. She's a fading image, like some old religious symbol I don't understand. And at those moments, Linda, I swear, I want to burn up every inch of tape until she's gone forever.

Pause.

LINDA   So, are you seeing anyone?

DIANE   Yes. Very good.

LINDA   Well, then. Who?

DIANE   I'm not telling. He's younger. Much younger.

LINDA   Good for you.

DIANE   Great for me.

LINDA   How are the boys?

DIANE   So-so. Russell is dropping out of graduate school at NYU and moving back to L.A. to "figure things out," whatever that means. He's brilliant—he writes, he directs. But he's restless. We're very much alike, which scares me.

LINDA   And what about . . . ?

DIANE   Adam. Adam is happy, so I don't hear from him. He's married, working for a computer firm in Oregon. He might as well be on Neptune. He hasn't made me a grandmother yet, so I thank God for small favors.

LINDA   Do you speak to their father?

DIANE   Never. Never at all.

LINDA   That's a shame.

DIANE   Why?

LINDA   Well, um . . . I'm the one who asks the questions.

DIANE   Yes, and you're so good at it, too. And I'd tell you to ask away, but, can you believe it, I'm out of time.

LINDA   Oh.

DIANE   Thank you for listening, Linda. I shouldn't have gone on like that. I guess my nerves are frayed. I go a little crazy when my life gets a little dull. I'm always hoping something momentous will happen. Something to shake things up. I'm sorry if I lost it.

LINDA   Not at all. And Diane, I won't print any of what you said. You know.

DIANE   Oh, fuck it, go ahead. No, you're right. Thank you. In fact, Linda, if you don't mind . . .

Diane opens the tape recorder and pulls out the tape. She breaks it in half against the table and puts the remains in her purse.

LINDA   What are you . . . ? You really don't have to . . .

DIANE   I know, but I'll feel better this way. Thank you, Linda. I needed this.

LINDA   I think something will happen, Diane. I feel it.

DIANE   Funny. I do too.

Diane exits. Linda's short musical sting plays and the lights change. Linda faces the audience and speaks her column.

LINDA   Thursday column. We spent a delightful lunch with the always radiant Diane Barrow at the Plaza this week. Diane was in New York hawking her sexy new workout video but she spent most of lunch discussing her family. As always, Diane is a mother first, superstar second. And if anyone forgets what made her a star, they can tune in her classic series every night on cable, a fact that thrills Diane to no end. And why not? She hasn't changed a bit. So, where are those film roles, Hollywood? Or maybe another series? From what I can tell, she's ready for anything.

Music: Linda's sting.

SCENE TWO

Lights up on a small coffee house in Los Feliz, California. PAM
GOLDMAN *enters to applause, carrying a microphone. She is in
her late twenties, warm but driven.* RUSSELL BURKE, *also late
twenties, neurotic and befuddled, sits watching.*

PAM Hi, it's me again! How are you all doing? Wow, what a
night! It has been such a thrill for me to be your host, here
at this fabulous new coffeehouse in Los Feliz—Java Nagila.
(*A neon sign that says "Java Nagila" lights up.*) Please tell all
your friends about our show, *Victims Know More.* (*The words
"Victims Know More" are projected on the wall.*) Boy, did you
ever think an evening of performance art by survivors of
abuse could be this much fun? The last three hours have just
flown by, haven't they? Who says we have no culture in
L.A.? God, such good work. Well, now it's my turn to
wrap things up. I'm a bit nervous because I have an old
boyfriend in the house tonight. Don't get jealous, Laura, it
was a long time ago. Love ya, honey. (*She blows Laura a
kiss.*) Yes, Russell is here, and that's exciting for two
reasons. One, because I love him, and two, he's related to
an important subject of my piece. The one, the only, Diane
Barrow. Yes. Russell is her son. Can you believe that?
Stand up, Russell. Don't be shy. Can we get a spot on him?
(*The spotlight shines on Russell, who is mortified.*) Diane
Barrow's son everybody! Okay, you can put the light back
on me. Thank you. God, Diane Barrow, wasn't she
fabulous? When I was growing up, I wanted to be Diane
Barrow. Or at least Diane Rogers, her character on *The
Diane Barrow Show.* Remember the opening credits? (*Music:
The Diane Barrow Show theme song. Pam mimes the opening
credit sequence—Diane at work, at home baking cookies, being
caught, and giving her signature wave and shrug. Pam speaks as*

the music continues:) A single mom with two adorable kids, flirting with her boss, Mr. Pratt, wearing calf-high leather boots. And if I couldn't, I wanted my mother to be Diane Barrow—I'd be Meg, her stupid blond daughter with the freckles, terrorized by big brother Jeremy, played by Kirby Phillips who wore his pants low on his hips—I noticed those things once. Before I desired Diane Barrow herself. (*The music ends.*) Yes, I desired Diane Barrow, I desired Diane Barrow—with her plucked eyebrows, her miniskirt, her fluffy, brunette . . . fall. I didn't care when my parents got divorced, when Mom started selling Xerox machines, because our family tragedy brought me closer to my dream. "It's all right Mommy, we'll be a family by ourselves. A single woman can go it alone, raise children, and find love and laughter along the way." But then came—Marty. Mom met Marty, and the party was over. (*The lights change and jazz music plays.*) He was a jazz musician, not a good one. Mom would be at work when I came home from school, but *Marty* would be there. *Marty* would be lying on the couch, *Marty* would be listening to standards on his eight-track hi-fi. *Marty* would ask me about my day, about that spelling test. I'd answer, feeling that tightness in my stomach. I knew that *Marty* would follow me into my room, that *Marty* would close the blinds and tell me to be quiet. "No, Marty, please." In the other room, Judy Garland sang "Do It Again." (*Pam nods to an unseen tech person. Nothing happens. In frustration, she turns and hisses, "Now!" A tape screeches on. Music: Judy Garland singing the chorus of "Do It Again." Speaking with Judy:*) "Oh, do it again. (*As young Pam:*) Please, don't, Marty. (*Ironically, with Judy:*) "I may say, 'No, no, no, no . . . Nooooo! Do it again! No one is near. I may cry oh, oh, oh, Nooooo! But no one can hear." No one ever hears! Not Marty, not

Mommy, not Judy, not even Diane Barrow! (*Music: The end of the TV show theme marks the end of her piece.*)   Thank you! Break the cycle! Good night!

Blackout on Pam. The sound of applause from the thirty or so people in the club. Russell is horrified. PAUL MICHAEL, thirty, gay, approaches him.

PAUL   Excuse me.

RUSSELL   I'm meeting a woman.

PAUL   Hello, Russell. It's Paul Michael. Your mother's assistant?

RUSSELL   Oh, God, hi. I'm sorry, it's been a while. What are you doing here?

PAUL   I had a friend in the show.

RUSSELL   Which one?

PAUL   Uncle Fred at the picnic, she sang "Mama, Look Sharp."

RUSSELL   Right. Why did she spread peanut butter on her . . . ?

PAUL   I have no idea. Well, we're both good friends to come.

RUSSELL   That's the trouble with living in the artistic community. You never know when a friend will invite you to his new theater group's production of *Marat/Sade*.

PAUL   Don't I know it. So, I'm doing a showcase next week, I hope you can come.

Pam enters and hugs Russell.

PAM   Hi, sweetie.

RUSSELL   There she is.

PAM   So were you surprised?

RUSSELL   You betcha. Pam Goldman, this is . . .

PAUL   Paul Michael. I'm Russell's mother's personal assistant.

PAM   Oh, my God! Did you see the show?

PAUL   Yes. (*Pause.*)   Well, I better get going. Welcome back, Russell. I hope you'll come over to the house. Your mother's been wondering where you are.

RUSSELL   I'll stop by. Tomorrow.

PAUL   Good. She's really worried about you. Bye.

Paul exits.

PAM   God, I'm so angry you were here the night the sound got screwed up.

RUSSELL   It didn't make any difference.

PAM   Really? Good. So, tell me what you thought.

RUSSELL   Did you have to do all that stuff about my mother?

PAM   It's a tribute. I think your mother is hot.

RUSSELL   Oh, stop, stop, eek.

PAM   Still pretty uptight, I see.

RUSSELL   If that means I don't like to hear my now lesbian ex-girlfriend lust after my mother, then yes, I'm uptight.

PAM   So, are you seeing anyone?

RUSSELL   No. I wouldn't wish myself on anybody right now.

PAM That's pathetic.

RUSSELL I know this sounds pretentious but I just feel it would be difficult to maintain a relationship during this period of artistic growth.

PAM As what kind of artist?

RUSSELL As a director or something.

PAM That's more specific than usual. How are you going about it?

RUSSELL I don't know.

PAM Well, whatever you do, don't start a theater company. The minute someone feels lost in this town, they start another theater company.

RUSSELL I'll try not to.

PAM Have you spoken to your mother?

RUSSELL Occasionally I get a word in.

PAM How long has it been?

RUSSELL We're just short of estranged.

PAM That's stupid. She can help you. I'm sure she still has plenty of contacts . . .

RUSSELL I don't need my mother!

PAM Sweetie, this whole country needs your mother.

RUSSELL All right, can we talk about something else?

PAM Okay. So, what did you think of my piece?

RUSSELL Oh, Pam, you don't want that.

PAM You hated it.

RUSSELL No, I'm just so sick of analyzing everything. That's why I finally left NYU. I can't experience anything anymore. I can't see a movie without picking the brilliant insights I'll have over capuccino by the third reel. I can't watch *Beavis and Butt-Head* without thinking of Beckett and Brecht. And I'm too well-read to ever believe I actually have an original thought in my brain. So I say, the hell with it, academia can deconstruct my ass. From now on, I'm just going to experience without interpreta-tion. I am against interpretation. But then I realize I'm just quoting Susan Sontag so I'm back in the same fucking place I started.

PAM God, you need therapy.

RUSSELL I do not. It's just the "anxiety of influence." My problem is aesthetic, not psychological.

PAM I'm not so sure. Sounds like you need to work through some heavy shit.

RUSSELL Here we go.

PAM If you're not in recovery, you're in denial.

RUSSELL Wow. That's the most offensive thing I've ever heard.

PAM Okay, that's a little extreme.

RUSSELL A little? Jesus. So to you everyone's either abused or abusing, is that it?

PAM No, not everyone. If you were listening to my piece, and you still haven't told me what you thought . . .

RUSSELL Pam, don't make me . . .

PAM   I can take it. Russell, I love you and I respect your opinion. Whatever you say won't hurt me. It will instruct me as an artist. Please,

RUSSELL   I'm really not a fan of performance art . . .

PAM   Please.

RUSSELL   All right. I liked the use of the Gershwin song. That was a sophisticated use of popular culture. It was as if you, the little girl, were being oppressed not only by Marty but by the entire society and its culture that denies the sexual autonomy of women.

PAM   Exactly. That is exactly what I was going for.

RUSSELL   That's the good news. As for the reenactment of the abuse, well, you didn't leave any perspective, any distance from the scene. You assume we, in the audience, share your outrage, right? And we're supposed to agree that these terrible things that happened explain the rage you feel in your adult life. Now, that may or may not be true, so you can't expect us to support you unconditionally. Then it's not performance, it's therapy. That's what I thought.

Pam is hurt.

PAM   Gee, thanks. Thanks a lot.

RUSSELL   I knew this would happen. You asked me what I thought.

PAM   Those are my feelings. I exposed something very personal and important to me. But you don't see that. Russell, I don't care what you think, how well you can explicate. I want to know how it affected you. How did it make you *feel?*

RUSSELL   It made me sad. It made me terribly sad.

219

Diane Barrow's office in her home. Paul enters, talking on the phone.

PAUL "Oh, do it again. I may cry no, no, *noooo!*" I swear to God, I'll never be able to listen to the Carnegie Hall album again . . . What could I do? The place was so tiny, I would have had to walk right by her to get to the door, and I figured she's already been through so much in her life . . . Anyway, that's not why I called. I'm doing a showcase. I'm in a scene from *The Vortex*. It's a play by Noël Coward but it's not funny. It's about a handsome, restless young man who's obsessed with his glamorous mother. So he shoots heroin. Of course, I think he's really gay . . . Not *always*. I *often* say that and I'm usually right. So will you come? It's next Thursday. (*From the bedroom, we hear a loud moan that expands into an abrupt yelp, ending in an exuberant "Yes!"*) Oh, dear. Did you hear that? I have to go. Madame is finally awake. Yes, she's very excited because Mr. DeMille loved her script for *Salomé*. I'll call you later.

Diane bursts into the room wearing a silk robe. She's had an eventful evening. Her hair is a mess.

DIANE God, what a gorgeous morning. Days like this we really should thank God.

PAUL Should I send a note or a gift basket? You're in Linda Simmons. Sounds like you two had a nice time at the Plaza.

DIANE (*She reads the column carefully.*) Well, Barbara Walters isn't interested. Linda will do for now. This is good.

PAUL Diane, it's excellent.

DIANE Linda writes best when she thinks you're falling apart. I gave her what she likes.

PAUL   Apparently. Sounds like she *wants* you.

DIANE   Oh, who doesn't?

PAUL   You're in a good mood. Did you and Taylor . . . ?
(*Off her smile.*)   Is he in there?

DIANE   No, I sent him home.

PAUL   I can't stand it! I'm never going to see him.

DIANE   Yes, you will. He's picking me up for lunch today.

PAUL   Thank you.

DIANE   Get us into The Ivy. We've entered a less secretive
phase. He wants it that way. Last night, we went to a party.
One of those evenings where everyone looks familiar. You
know, you're sure you know them from television or life
but they didn't make a very strong impression in either.

PAUL   And how did it go?

DIANE   Taylor was charming. He got a little too chummy
with some casting directors for my taste. But no major
gaffes. I was proud of my boy. Paul, I think I may be in
love with him. Oh God, don't let me become one of those
pathetic, deluded older women.

PAUL   That'll never happen.

DIANE   I'd better get ready. What time is it?

PAUL   Noon. Hurry, you look terrible.

DIANE (*She hurries toward the bedroom.*)   Thelma Ritter never
spoke to her bosses that way.

PAUL   Yes she did. Oh, I ran into Russell last night.

Diane stops and turns around.

DIANE You did? How is he?

PAUL All right, I guess. He's coming by.

DIANE (*Urgent*) When?

PAUL Today, I think.

RUSSELL (*From offstage*) Hello? Mom? (*Diane rushes off to the bedroom. Russell enters.*) Oh, hi.

PAUL Hello again. Your mom just got up. She's dressing for a lunch date.

RUSSELL (*Glancing at his watch*) She's not going to sell too many low-impact workout videos sleeping till noon.

PAUL Well, she had a big night last night.

RUSSELL Really? Doing what?

PAUL Her lunch date. Never mind. So, I'm curious, what made you move back to L.A.?

RUSSELL I don't know. I was in this program at NYU Performance Studies.

PAUL What's that?

RUSSELL No one knows. I asked. No one could tell me. "It's the study of performance" was the best anyone could do. Two months ago, I handed in a proposal for my dissertation: "Next Window to Moscow: Allegories of Waiting As Seen in the Plays of Anton Chekhov and the Department of Motor Vehicles."

PAUL Was it accepted?

RUSSELL They offered me a grant. I knew it was time to leave.

PAUL Well, you're lucky to be out of there.

RUSSELL You think so?

PAUL Absolutely. This is your home.

TAYLOR (*From offstage*) Hello?

PAUL Welcome home.

TAYLOR McDONALD *enters. He doesn't look much older than Russell. He is also stunningly handsome.*

TAYLOR Hey. Uh, is Diane here?

PAUL Oh, my. Hello. I'm Paul.

TAYLOR Oh, hi.

PAUL This is Russell. And this is Taylor. Your mother's lunch date.

RUSSELL Oh. Hi.

PAUL I love this job.

TAYLOR I've heard a lot about you.

RUSSELL I've heard nothing about you.

TAYLOR Well, your mom wants to keep our relationship a little quiet. I think she's afraid it might damage my career.

RUSSELL You're an actor?

TAYLOR You bet. Diane doesn't want me to get stuck in her shadow.

RUSSELL That's probably best.

TAYLOR Your mom's a great lady.

RUSSELL Thank you. I know.

TAYLOR   I hope this isn't awkward for you.

RUSSELL   Oh, no. Not really. Over the years, Mom has dated lots of men. Of course, she's gotten older and they've stayed the same age.

TAYLOR   Yeah, well. Good. It's really great you have such a positive attitude.

RUSSELL   That's me.

TAYLOR   (*Joking*)   And it's not like I expect you to call me Dad or anything.

RUSSELL   Have no fear.

TAYLOR   Cool. This isn't awkward at all.

Pause. Diane enters. She looks fantastic. She carries jewelry that she will put on during the scene.

DIANE   There's my beautiful boy! (*Both Russell and Taylor turn and rise. To Taylor, intimate:*)   Good morning. (*To Russell:*)   Russell, you look tired. Are you all settled in? How's the new place?

RUSSELL   Everything's fine.

DIANE   You have enough money? I can put more in the account.

RUSSELL   (*Embarrassed*)   No, I'm fine. Ma, please.

DIANE   So, you've met Taylor. Isn't he wonderful?

TAYLOR   Diane, stop. Russ doesn't have to . . .

RUSSELL   He's very nice. And it's Russell, not Russ.

TAYLOR   Sorry.

DIANE He's oversensitive. Will you help me with that, sweetie? (*She turns her back to Taylor, who fastens her necklace.*) So, you're here, you're back. What are you doing?

RUSSELL I don't know yet. I'm figuring things out.

DIANE (*Dubious*) Hmm.

RUSSELL I am. I'll probably do some theater.

DIANE Well, that always sounds nice.

RUSSELL Do you remember Pam? She's out here. She's a performance artist.

DIANE Pam is? No kidding. I always liked her.

RUSSELL She always liked you, too.

DIANE Well, good. Just do something. Don't sit around and think. You've always been a thinker.

RUSSELL I know, I know.

DIANE My son is overeducated.

RUSSELL That's a laugh.

DIANE It's true. You must be ashamed of your old mother and her boob-tube career.

TAYLOR You're not old.

DIANE Thank you, Taylor.

RUSSELL How could I be ashamed of you? You're a national treasure. You're part of our "television heritage," which is all that's left. If T. S. Eliot were writing today, *The Waste Land* would be full of cryptic allusions to *My Mother the Car* and *Petticoat Junction*.

PAUL And *The Diane Barrow Show.*

DIANE Well, that's depressing.

RUSSELL We don't have a culture anymore. We have pastiche. I'm proud you're a part of it.

DIANE You're sweet. I want you to be happy.

RUSSELL And how do I do that?

DIANE Get busy.

RUSSELL Is that the answer?

DIANE Absolutely. Look at me. I've got the workout video. And I'm in talks with NBC about a movie-of-the-week. I'm going to remake *Mildred Pierce*. Nobody's ever done it except for the first time. It'll be fabulous. Taylor is going to play Monty.

PAUL And I'm playing Veda.

DIANE No, you're not. You're not going to play my daughter, Paul, and that's final.

PAUL Of course not. We make Veda Mildred's son, Vito. Then one night she finds him in bed with Monty, her new playboy husband. She's horrified, what mother wouldn't be? But when Vito shoots Monty in a lover's quarrel in their Malibu beach house, Mildred lies to protect her gay son. It's the perfect modern twist. The ratings will go through the roof.

DIANE No.

PAUL Think about it.

TAYLOR Wait a minute, isn't *my* character named Monty?

DIANE Don't listen to him, sweetheart. All right, let's eat.

TAYLOR   You look beautiful.

DIANE   God, you're gorgeous. Russell, look at this. Look at this stomach. (*She pulls up Taylor's shirt and makes a raspberry sound with her mouth against his stomach.*)   I used to do that to you when you were a little boy.

PAUL (*Into the phone*)   Paging Dr. Freud? Dr. Freud, you're needed immediately.

DIANE   You make me happy, Taylor. Even if this doesn't last very long.

TAYLOR   Why do you say things like that? I'm serious about this. I want more of you. I want to see you when you wake up in the morning.

DIANE   No, you don't.

TAYLOR   Yes, I do.

RUSSELL & PAUL   No, you don't.

DIANE   Let's get out of here. Paul, did you make a reservation?

PAUL   Yes.

DIANE   Make it now. Russell, would you like to join us?

RUSSELL   No thanks.

DIANE   Don't get too thin. You'll end up like your brother, a scarecrow sitting in front of a computer screen. Have you heard from him?

RUSSELL   Not for a while.

DIANE   Oh well, he has a life. Don't worry about a thing, Russell. You'll pull yourself together. I have every faith in you. I'll make a few calls . . .

227

RUSSELL I don't need you . . . !

DIANE Fine. Whatever you want. Let me know what happens. Taylor?

TAYLOR Bye, guys.

DIANE Move it.

Diane and Taylor exit.

PAUL (*Suddenly intense, with a British accent*) "Now then! Now then! You're not going to have any more lovers; you're not going to be beautiful and successful ever again— you're going to be my mother for once—it's about time I had one to help me, before I go over the edge altogether!"

RUSSELL What is that?

PAUL It's Noël Coward. But it's not funny.

RUSSELL No. It's not.

Scene Four

A therapist's office. DR. MARGARET THURM *enters and addresses Russell.*

MARGARET I should tell you before we start that Pam has talked to me about you. So I know who your mother is.

RUSSELL Well, it seems everyone does. (*Margaret smiles and writes something down on a pad. Russell tries to see what it is.*) I didn't mean that in a hostile way. I just spend so much of my life meeting fans of my mother's. It's a reflex.

MARGARET I didn't say I was a fan.

RUSSELL Oh. You're the one. What do you have against my mother?

MARGARET Nothing. Nothing at all.

RUSSELL Because I know a lot of women resent her. There she was, this attractive single mom with an important job. Able to solve personal and professional problems in twenty-two minutes (with the exception of the occasional two-parter). Millions of women aspired to duplicate her character's success. The fact that they all failed and their kids hate them isn't really Mom's fault. You can't blame her for their feelings of inadequacy any more than you can blame Mother Theresa. Of course, no one actually wants to *be* Mother Theresa.

MARGARET Let's talk about you. About why you're here. (*Off Russell's blank stare.*) You first.

RUSSELL Okay. I just can't seem to get started. I feel like I'm trapped in a waiting room. Waiting for, I don't know what. Godot maybe. Or some kindly nurse to open the office door and say, "Russell Burke, the world will see you now." I feel paralyzed, I feel like a failure. I don't want to feel that way. Now, I know you're going to say it's because of my childhood but I don't think so. My childhood was very nice. I think my problem has more to do with my sense of identity.

MARGARET Meaning?

RUSSELL I'm not sure I have one. Or maybe it just seems that way to me because I have unrealistic expectations. That's just my theory.

MARGARET Sounds like you've got it all figured out.

RUSSELL No, do I? No, I really don't. I told my mother that's why I moved back, to figure things out. She's paying for these sessions. Technically. I mean, she doesn't know it yet but she is. But anyway, I really don't want to talk about her.

MARGARET All right.

RUSSELL I don't mean to be defensive.

MARGARET That's fine.

RUSSELL But it's such a cliché, isn't it? To sit here and whine about Mom. My mother is who she is. She's insane but I love her. Doesn't everyone feel that way about their parents? They're lovable nuts?

MARGARET I don't know.

Russell stares at her, resentful.

RUSSELL Well, that's what I think. So, I really didn't come here to rehash my childhood.

MARGARET Why did you come here?

RUSSELL Because I'm unhappy now. Right? That's why. That and because I can't sleep. (*Beat.*)   I can't sleep. I just can't. And when I do, I don't dream. At least, I don't remember after. It's been months now and I'm going a little wacko, you know?

MARGARET Why do you think you don't dream?

RUSSELL I don't know. Look, Pam swears by you, so I figured I'd give you a shot. But I'm telling you, I am not interested in dredging up some god-awful image of being beaten with a wire hanger. (*Dr. Thurm writes in her pad. Russell starts to leave.*)   You know what? Forget it. This isn't going to work.

MARGARET You may be right. You may have had a perfect childhood. Maybe you're the one. I'm not offering you any easy answers and I would never put ideas in your head. If we work together, it will mean hard work, absolute truthfulness, and an impossibly open mind. But if we're successful, and that's a big if, the process can deliver you to a new state of being. You will sleep and you will dream. Would you like that?

SCENE FIVE

Bernini, a men's clothing store on Rodeo Drive. Russell shops for tuxedos with Diane's help.

DIANE This is fun. It reminds me of when you were little, taking you for new clothes every fall.

RUSSELL I don't remember that. I don't remember you taking me. I remember Dad once . . .

DIANE Why do you want to hurt me? I took you. I did.

RUSSELL I'm sure. I just remember Dad losing his patience once and pissing off the salesman.

DIANE Oh, that's all right then.

RUSSELL (*Frustrated in his search*) Oh, I don't know. I can never decide.

DIANE You want help? I can ask André.

RUSSELL No, I want to do it myself. I don't know why you want me to go. Isn't that Taylor's job?

DIANE It wouldn't be smart. I don't want everyone at the Emmys talking about me. Well, I do but not about that. And Taylor doesn't want people to think of him as some plaything. He's an actor, a good one.

RUSSELL Really?

DIANE   Oh, who knows? We'll have fun. It will lift you out of this funk or whatever it is. I worry about you.

RUSSELL   I know you do. Thanks.

He holds up a tuxedo.

DIANE   That one's stunning.

RUSSELL   I'll try it. (*He takes it off the hanger and fusses before a mirror.*)   Mom, I've started seeing a therapist.

DIANE   Oh, God. Why?

RUSSELL   You just said it yourself. I'm in a "funk," or something. And I'm having trouble sleeping.

DIANE   Take a pill. I'll call Dr. Weisman.

RUSSELL   I want to try this first.

He models the tuxedo jacket for her.

DIANE   I don't like it.

RUSSELL   Why not?

DIANE   You're expecting strangers to fix things for you.

RUSSELL   I don't expect her to fix anything. I don't know if I trust her, to tell you the truth. I think it will be an interesting process for me. It will help me focus.

DIANE   Focus on what?

RUSSELL   Well, we're starting on my childhood.

DIANE   Of course you are. She'll tell you I'm a monster, I'm sure of it.

RUSSELL   She doesn't tell me anything. We're just looking at my feelings.

DIANE If you ask me, everything fell apart when people got the idea that what really mattered were their feelings. I can't tell you how many friends I've seen go through years and years of analysis and come out loopier than they were before. And they were actors.

RUSSELL So I take it you never sought counseling.

DIANE Never.

RUSSELL Even during the divorce? Or when the show got canceled?

DIANE What for? I look forward, Rusty, only forward, never back.

RUSSELL Yeah, but if you don't look back, how do you know who you are?

DIANE I watch what I do next. You look like a maître d'. Try another one.

Russell smiles and searches for another tuxedo jacket.

RUSSELL You're amazing.

DIANE No.

RUSSELL Yes, you are. I'm in awe of you sometimes.

DIANE You shouldn't be. We're exactly alike.

RUSSELL We are?

DIANE We're both restless, needy people. The trouble is, you haven't learned to use that to your advantage. But you will.

RUSSELL How did you do it?

DIANE My Aunt Julie. She taught me the greatest lesson in life.

RUSSELL Tell me.

DIANE It was after I didn't make it into the Honor Society in high school and I was very upset. Aunt Julie sat me down and said, "Deedee, through your life, you will meet girls who are smarter than you, but you will be prettier. And then there will be girls who are prettier than you, but you will be smarter."

RUSSELL But what about . . . ?

DIANE Well, I asked. I said, "But Aunt Julie, what about girls who are both smarter and prettier than I am?"

RUSSELL What'd she say?

DIANE She said, "Don't pay any attention to them, they're freaks." So I never did. And I had two Emmys and God knows how much money by the time I was thirty-five.

RUSSELL That's a touching story, Mom.

DIANE Try this one.

She hands him another tuxedo jacket.

RUSSELL Sometimes I think, look at Adam. Lucky Adam, content with his PC in Oregon.

DIANE No. Lucky us. We're in the game. The big one. Don't stay on the sidelines, kiddo. Put on your cleats and your cup and play. It's a helluva lot more fun.

RUSSELL You should do seminars, you know that? You're really good.

DIANE I'm better than some shrink, that's for sure. So, how is it going with Dr. Feelings?

RUSSELL Not very well. I can't seem to remember anything interesting.

Diane grabs Russell's shoulders and dusts the latest jacket. She approves.

DIANE Wonderful! There's my beautiful boy! (*She kisses him on the lips.*) I got myself the hottest date in town.

SCENE SIX

Dr. Thurm's office.

MARGARET "Beautiful boy."

RUSSELL She always called me her "beautiful boy." I was a cute kid.

MARGARET How did that make you feel?

RUSSELL Special. Loved. I don't know, attractive.

MARGARET Attractive.

RUSSELL Sure. I wish I felt that way now.

MARGARET You don't feel attractive now.

RUSSELL Not especially.

MARGARET But you did then.

RUSSELL Not in a sexual way. But think about it. Every kid knows his mother loves him, well, except for the horror stories. And maybe a third know they're Mom's favorite. Well, I was Mom's favorite and my mom was a star. Hmm. (*He thinks to himself and smiles.*) I just remembered something.

MARGARET Yes?

RUSSELL Something wonderful. One night when I was growing up. It was parent-teacher night in junior high

school. Adam and I were in our pajamas early. Mrs.
Kennedy made us chocolate milk with Bosco for a treat.

As Russell tells his memory, the lights change and fragments of what he describes are reenacted around him.

MARGARET   Who?

RUSSELL   Mrs. Kennedy. She was our maid. Mom always used to joke she had a Kennedy working in the kitchen.

MARGARET   (*As* MRS. KENNEDY)   Boys, drink up now and get ready for bed. Come on, Adam, Russell, don't make me ask you twice. (*As herself again:*)   Hold on. What are you doing?

RUSSELL   I'm sorry. You remind me of her.

MARGARET   Oh, no. I don't play domestics.

RUSSELL   She was a very nice woman.

MARGARET   I didn't go to school for ten years to become your maid.

RUSSELL   Please.

Margaret relents. She rises and assumes the role of Mrs. Kennedy.

MRS. KENNEDY   Boys, let's get washed up now. Your parents will be home soon. Don't forget to brush your teeth.

RUSSELL   I won't.

MARGARET   How old were you?

RUSSELL   I don't know. Twelve. Eleven.

MRS. KENNEDY   And Russell, I want you asleep by eleven.

RUSSELL   No chance. Not on PTA night. I was bouncing off the ceiling. Adam teased me. He was already a freshman in high school and didn't care. He just went to his room and read another Robert Heinlein sci-fi novel. But I couldn't calm down. All I could think about was my mom at school. Dazzling the teachers. Dazzling my friends' parents. I knew that everyone would treat me a little bit differently for the next week or so, now that they'd been reminded where I came from. And I knew that Mom would be home soon and we'd talk about it in my room.

Diane appears with her husband at the time, STAN BURKE, *Jewish, harried.*

DIANE   Hello, Mrs. Kennedy. Were they any trouble?

MRS. KENNEDY   Not at all. Russell's a bit excited . . .

DIANE   Is he?

MRS. KENNEDY   How were the teachers?

STAN   Imbeciles. All of them. We'd be better off having you teach them all day, Mrs. Kennedy.

MRS. KENNEDY   That goes without saying.

Stan exits.

DIANE   Where's Russell, in his room?

MRS. KENNEDY   Waiting up for you, I bet.

RUSSELL   And then she'd appear in the doorway. A whole country's dream of "mother" in my doorway. Looking beautiful and radiant and . . . real.

DIANE   You asleep?

RUSSELL   Not really. How was it?

DIANE   Well, I don't know how you stand those people all day.

RUSSELL   Mom! You say that every year.

They laugh together. Diane sits next to Russell.

DIANE   I liked Mr. Fleming, the science teacher.

RUSSELL   *Eeew,* you liked Mr. Phlegm? He's so gross.

DIANE   He spoke highly of you.

Stan enters.

STAN   Hey, Rusty, what are you doing up?

RUSSELL   Hi, Dad.

STAN   Your teachers like you, you're doing good. I'm gonna eat something, Deedee, you want anything?

DIANE   No thanks. Don't talk to yourself, it drives me crazy.

STAN   I'm gonna make a sandwich. (*Stan walks off absentmindedly. Diane and Russell look at each other and count to three. Stan mutters to himself as he exits.*)   Network *schmucks.* I'm executive producer, I gotta worry about the friggin' bumpers. Unbelievable.

Diane and Russell laugh together.

RUSSELL   He always did that. That's when he drank. At least, I think so, I was upstairs with Mom. (*Back to Diane.*) What did you think of Miss Carter, my English teacher? Wasn't she nice?

DIANE   She's all right. Pretty.

RUSSELL   She's my favorite.

DIANE   I thought I was your favorite.

RUSSELL You know what I mean.

DIANE I know. There's my beautiful boy.

She pulls up Russell's shirt and makes a raspberry sound with her mouth against his stomach. He giggles.

RUSSELL We joked and talked. We listened to my father muttering to himself. Adam complained that we were keeping him awake and we felt bad for a minute but then we laughed some more. That's all I remember.

MARGARET Okay.

RUSSELL She kissed me good night.

MARGARET She kissed you.

Diane kisses Russell's cheek.

RUSSELL I think so, on the cheek.

MARGARET Keep going.

Diane kisses Russell on the mouth.

RUSSELL Maybe on the mouth. I'm not sure.

MARGARET Keep going.

RUSSELL She was lying on the bed next to me. I could smell her, I think it was White Shoulders. That's what she wore.

MARGARET It's late now.

RUSSELL Yes. Adam's asleep. Dad's downstairs.

MARGARET Your mother is next to you.

RUSSELL Yes. It's exciting. To have her so close. I'm happy. She says something.

MARGARET She says . . .

RUSSELL Wait. I can hear her. She's reaching for me. She's saying . . .

DIANE "Years from now . . . when you talk about this . . . and you will . . . be kind."

The lights change. Diane walks offstage.

RUSSELL That's not it, is it?

MARGARET I doubt it.

RUSSELL What do you think this means?

MARGARET Well, clearly, your relationship with your mother had great impact on your development.

RUSSELL No kidding. Boy, I'm disappointed.

MARGARET I'm sorry?

RUSSELL Well, I tell you a vague memory of being close to my mother and you tell me it's about me being close to my mother. What about Freud's theory of displacement?

MARGARET What about it?

RUSSELL Shouldn't you be in interpretive mode? Aren't the marginal details more important? All right, this technically wasn't a dream—I don't *have* dreams, I can't sleep—but still. Maybe Mrs. Kennedy is the key. The whole thing could be about the failure of modern liberalism.

MARGARET We're out of time.

RUSSELL Oh.

MARGARET Russell, therapy is not a science, it's an art. We are trying, the best we can, to find whatever is keeping you under a cloud of neurotic unhappiness. I think it would be wise for us not to ignore the most obvious clues thrown our way.

RUSSELL   Meaning I was in bed with my mother.

MARGARET   We'll pick it up from there. See you next time.

RUSSELL   Dr. Thurm, Margaret . . . I don't think I want to continue. I don't want to pursue this any further.

MARGARET   Oh. Well, that's your choice. I'm sorry to hear it. You're uncomfortable, Russell, because you're moving toward a difficult place.

RUSSELL   Yeah. Well, I don't want to go there.

MARGARET   What about your insomnia?

RUSSELL   I'll take a pill.

SCENE SEVEN

Diane is by her pool, talking on her cell phone. On the other side of the stage, we see HELEN MENKEN, Diane's agent, answering her office phone during a busy day.

HELEN   (*A phony voice*) Helen Menken's office.

DIANE   Is she there please?

HELEN   Who's calling?

DIANE   Diane Barrow. I swear.

HELEN   (*Her real voice*) Diane, how are you, sweetheart? It's me, Helen. I don't have an assistant, I'm answering my own goddamn phone.

DIANE   What happened to Robin?

HELEN   The bitch sold a screenplay. Some action/feminist/violent/space thing. I could kill her. I walk into my office and she's spread the trades out with the stories about the sale in yellow highlighter and she's dancing around singing, "Free at last, free at last, thank God almighty, I'm free at last." And this is a Jewish girl. Now is that right?

DIANE   Of course not.

HELEN   She went to another agency. The slut. I'm thinking of bad-mouthing her but I don't do that.

DIANE   That's good to know.

HELEN   So I'll have to train someone. Does Russell have any interest in being an agent? I could put him on the fast track. He'd be off my desk in two years tops.

DIANE   I think Russell has grander ambitions right now.

HELEN   Well, excuse me.

DIANE   Helen . . .

HELEN   The two of you looked gorgeous at the Emmys. I've been getting calls.

DIANE   Really? Well, good. I . . .

HELEN   Wait just a second, Di. (*Calling off.*)   WHAT? All right. Give me a minute. GIVE ME A MINUTE. Christ. (*Back to Diane.*)   I have to go in a minute. Fucking Disney. Everything has to be done this second. But if you call them, they put you on hold for an hour while they play "Zip-a-Dee-Doo-Dah" in your ear. Diane, where are you, by the pool?

DIANE Yes. I wanted to check in since I haven't heard from you.

HELEN And you should. Listen, I'm glad I got you. ABC is looking to do another retrospective, a reunion with casts of your favorite shows, that kind of thing. They want to get you together with the kid who played your son . . .

DIANE Kirby Phillips? Isn't he in jail?

HELEN I don't know. If he is, the network will get him out. They're shooting for the spring.

DIANE Helen, how many times do I have to tell you? I'm tired of the retrospectives. I want to do something new. I want to do *Mildred Pierce*!

HELEN We're working on it. You're in a difficult place right now, Diane. Most of these snot-nosed kids who run everything grew up on you. They idolize you. They tell me, she's too glamorous. We don't want her in a TV movie with a stolen crack baby.

DIANE And what do you tell them?

HELEN I fight for you, kid. God, how I fight. But it's like Desert Storm and I'm a Kurd. You know what I'm saying?

DIANE What about Barbara Walters? Have you and Pete even called?

Taylor, fresh from a swim, joins Diane by the pool.

HELEN Nobody's interested. What can I tell you? But, listen, look at it this way. You're too good for them. They want weakness, they want sleaze, they want bad hair. And you have something they don't want. You know what that is, darling? Class.

DIANE Gee, I feel so much better.

HELEN That's what I'm here for, sweetheart.

DIANE Oh, is that it? That's funny, I thought you were here to get me a fucking job.

HELEN Diane, you're breaking up. The cell phone . . .

DIANE Fuck class. Fuck those snot-nosed kids. And fuck you.

HELEN Sorry. I can't hear you.

DIANE I don't care what I have to do. I'm going to work again. If you're not the one to help me, then I'll find some other parasite.

HELEN These damn cellular things. I hear they give you brain tumors, too. Deedee, I'm running to my meeting anyway.

Lights out on Helen as she hangs up.

DIANE Well, that was productive.

TAYLOR You'd think these people would remember who you were.

DIANE (*Slapping his stomach*) "Are," sweetheart, "are."

TAYLOR Ow, that hurt. Are.

DIANE Sorry. Pet peeve. Anyway, they do remember me, that's the problem.

TAYLOR How do you mean?

DIANE They're obsessed with me twenty years ago. I tell them I can be whatever they want, I'm an actress.

TAYLOR Good point.

DIANE No, they know I'm bluffing. Who knows if I'm any good anymore? And I'm not about to sit in some acting class doing scenes from *The Gingerbread Lady* to find out.

TAYLOR You're a great actress. You were brilliant on your show.

DIANE (*Slapping him again*) And all the kids in high school said so.

TAYLOR Ow. I never said that.

DIANE No, it's no use. I'm stuck for now. I can't be Diane Rogers . . . (*She makes a quick Diane Rogers wave/shrug gesture.*) because I don't believe she ever existed. She sure as shit doesn't now. It would be like me asking Russell why he's become such a sad sack. He was such a delicious child, so free, happy, open. How did he mess it all up? But then we all have those questions buzzing around our ears, don't we?

TAYLOR Not yet. (*Beat.*) Russell doesn't like me.

DIANE Of course he does.

TAYLOR Diane, give me a little credit.

DIANE Well, all right. So? Who cares? I like you. I like you a lot.

TAYLOR (*Pulling away, putting his shirt back on*) But it matters, Diane. I mean, ultimately, it does matter. If Russell still didn't like me, you would never . . . things could only go so far. And I'm starting to think you prefer it that way. I don't know . . .

DIANE Taylor, don't say things you don't mean.

TAYLOR Don't treat me like a child. Just don't, all right? Look, I'm younger than you are. I know that. Fine. The whole world knows that. But no one seems to care as much as you do. Christ, you can't say three words without bringing it up. I'm tired of it.

DIANE I didn't know. I'm sorry.

TAYLOR It's just . . . I'm not a toy, Diane. I'm not. I'm just a guy who's banging around, trying to put together a life that doesn't feel like waste of time, which isn't very easy to do in this business. You know what I mean?

DIANE (*Moved, excited by him*) Yes I do.

TAYLOR I'm still eager and I still have feelings. That's important. Look, I think you need me, Di. I can help you remember who you are. Because I remember. You're a sexy, exciting woman. That's why I'm here. Now, if that's not what you want, then I'll go. And we'll call it quits.

DIANE Well, my love. I certainly picked a winner in you.

TAYLOR (*Smiling*) Yeah. And don't you forget it.

DIANE Come here, you beautiful boy.

SCENE EIGHT

Java Nagila. Russell performs his own performance art piece. Pam watches him.

RUSSELL Today, I am a victim. *Ich bin ein* victim. For too long, I ignored the evidence. I mistook my own personal failings for my own personal failings. But no. I am a victim. I am the victim of a happy past. I am a white male who appreciates Western European culture, who believes the Renaissance was a magical moment in the history of art, that Ancient Greece was the birthplace of democracy. I am the victim of a happy past. I am heterosexual, though it's so impossible to have sex nowadays, that hardly seems relevant. I am of average height and body weight, my looks are passable. No earring in my nose, not the tiniest tattoo for which I am denied the good table at Denny's. I am white, straight, average. I am, therefore, tragically, uninteresting. Incapable of protest, of passion, of saying, "Mozart is dead fucking shit, man." I'm straight, but I dated a lesbian. I'm Gentile, but half-Jewish. I'm stuffy, but sympathetic to multicultural concerns. What am I to do? I must be a victim somehow, that is the currency of acceptance, the knock on the door to all the cool places, the whispered "Joe sent me" that allows one into the inner fold. My answer: I am the victim of a happy past. (*Music: Mozart's* Elvira Madigan Piano Concerto.)   Pretty, isn't it? They don't write 'em like that anymore. Some say I'm misreading the signs. I must be the victim of something else. Look closely, they say, you'll find the seeds of terror. So I lie awake and I look. My father drank. He did! But he never hit me. Damn, thought I had something there. And what of my mother? My famous, sexy mother? She's not only my past, she's your past too. What did she do to me? She would come to my room. She would lie on my bed. She would kiss me. She would kiss my naked backside. What else? Did she hit me? Well, maybe once she beaned me with an Emmy award. Who knows? What if there's more? Was there a cult? Was I fed dead babies by Satanists in robes in our Brentwood backyard? Am I doomed to cry real tears to Geraldo because he's the only one brave enough to believe me?

247

What will I find? Dare I look closer? Nooooo! (*The music stops. Lights change.*) I am afraid. But not of what I might find. I am afraid I won't find enough. Can there be anything terrible enough to explain the mess I'm making now? Yes, I am the victim of a happy past. I am America. (*Music: an up-tempo song from a classic American musical. Russell looks up in terror, then covers his ears.*) Nooooooo! (*The music stops, the piece is over.*) Thank you.

The lights fade. Scattered, unenthusiastic applause. Pam doesn't clap. Russell joins her. She is furious.

PAM   I can't believe you.

RUSSELL   I know, it needs work.

PAM   What has happened to you? Have you no shame? No sensitivity?

RUSSELL   All right, Pam, don't wig out.

PAM   You go up there and mock everything we do. You have no right! People have been hurt, Russell. Terrible things have been done to them, unforgivable things.

RUSSELL   Of course. I don't deny . . .

PAM   You've had a charmed life? You've never been a victim? Well, good for you but shut up, we don't want to hear about it! Is this out of spite? Is it because I don't love you anymore? Because I have a girlfriend?

RUSSELL   Give me a break. I auditioned. They thought it would be interesting to explore another side.

PAM   They thought it would be interesting to have Diane Barrow's son shoot his mouth off. That's why they let you spew forth like that. They wanted the publicity.

RUSSELL Publicity?

PAM Yes, Russell. The press. The press was here.

Lights out on them and up on Linda Simmons. Music: Linda's sting.

LINDA Monday column. In journalism school, they taught us the one claim that can damage someone more than any other is the claim of child abuse. I was reminded of this fact when word came in from my colleagues in L.A. of such a claim against one of TV's most beloved stars. Diane Barrow's son, Russell, her handsome escort at this year's Emmy awards, spoke of being abused physically and sexually by his mother in a recent performance at Java Nagila, a trendy new "coffee space" (and the latest brat-pack living room of choice). Russell listed all sorts of inappropriate behavior including a time Diane hit him with one of her well-deserved Emmy awards. It's always a shame to see ungrateful Hollywood children turn on their parents in such a public way. Especially with a tale as hard to believe as this one. We'll keep you posted as the sordid story unfolds.

Music: Linda's sting.

Scene Nine

Diane's home. It is morning and she has just read Linda Simmons's column which she holds in her hands. Paul stands frozen, unsure of what to do.

DIANE Noooooooo! No, no! It can't be . . . How . . . ?
Why . . . ?

PAUL I called Russell and got his machine. I'll keep trying.

DIANE Why is he betraying me? What have I ever done?

PAUL I don't know.

DIANE To put out these lies . . . They are lies, Paul! You know that, don't you?

PAUL Diane, you do not have to defend yourself to me.

DIANE But you know none of this is true.

PAUL If you say they're lies, I am inclined to believe you.

DIANE Oh, my God.

PAUL Please, let's not have this conversation. I'm standing by you. I am.

DIANE This could ruin me. Everything I've worked for. Everything I've planned. It could all be over. Over!

Taylor runs in. Diane falls in his arms.

TAYLOR I came the minute I heard.

DIANE Oh, Taylor. Thank God, you came.

PAUL That's really sweet.

DIANE Did you read it?

TAYLOR Actually, no, not yet. People called me.

DIANE Who called you?

TAYLOR Lisa, my ex-girlfriend.

DIANE Of course.

TAYLOR And my mother.

DIANE Oh, God. Why is this happening?

PAUL I don't know.

TAYLOR   I do. It's because of Russell. He's an ungrateful shithead. I'm gonna punch his face in, Diane. To say something like that, even if it's true . . .

DIANE   *It's not true!*

TAYLOR   Right, but what I'm saying . . .

Russell runs in.

RUSSELL   I can explain.

TAYLOR   This I've got to hear.

DIANE   Are you trying to kill me? Couldn't you just run me over with a car? Put poison in my cobb salad? Anything else? Have you read Linda Simmons? *Have you read Linda Simmons?!*

RUSSELL   Yes, I did. It's all a mistake. I never said those things. I mean, I did but I was misunderstood. It was all part of a parody. It was satire, I swear it.

TAYLOR   That's stupid.

RUSSELL   I was making a point.

DIANE   Well, very well done, sweetheart. You're a regular Larry Gelbart, you are.

RUSSELL   You have to believe me.

TAYLOR   Don't let him off the hook that easy.

DIANE   Shut up, Taylor. All right, Russell, say I do believe you. Now what? Huh, genius? What do we do now?

RUSSELL   Right. What now? Look, you could just call Pete and put out a statement.

PAUL He and Helen have got everybody from both coasts calling, waiting for something.

DIANE (*Feverish, sarcastic*) Great. Lovely. Paul, take this down, "I am not a child molester." There, that should do it. Russell, you've got to explain to everybody. And it better be convincing.

RUSSELL All right. Whatever you want.

DIANE Oh, thank God. Paul?

PAUL I'll call them right now. If we don't act fast, this thing will get huge.

Paul starts to dial. Beat. Diane thinks.

DIANE Hmm.

PAUL (*Into phone*) Pete?

DIANE Paul.

PAUL Hold on a minute.

RUSSELL What are you thinking?

DIANE On the other hand, people just love this kind of story nowadays, don't they?

RUSSELL Yes, they do. That was my point.

DIANE Well, then, why don't we have a little fun?

PAUL Pete? I'll call you back.

DIANE Maybe we can make something out of this.

TAYLOR Diane, I can't believe you'd even consider . . .

DIANE Oh, what have I got to lose, right? My career is in the shitter.

TAYLOR   That is not true.

DIANE   Yes it is. Now, this is what we do. Let the media speculate, jump through hoops for a few days.

RUSSELL   Then we appear, you and me, on any show we want probably, and together, we show them all.

DIANE   I could be interviewed.

RUSSELL   I could perform my piece.

DIANE   We'll see about that. Paul, tell Pete I'm not ready to speak to anyone.

PAUL   Right.

DIANE   Russell, you should leave. We can't be on close speaking terms. But you call me, we'll prepare. You can write something, you're such a wonderful writer.

RUSSELL   Good thinking. I really think, well, yes.

DIANE   And Russell, you see the sacrifice I'm making for you. The risks I'm taking. You can see how much I love you.

RUSSELL   Yes. I can, Mom. I love you, too.

DIANE   I'm proud of you, sweetheart. You're in the game. Now go.

Russell exits. Diane turns and smiles at Taylor.

TAYLOR   I am totally appalled. I mean, is this how it's done? Is this really how it's done?

DIANE   I have no idea, but we'll give it a shot.

Diane rereads Linda's column as she exits.

PAUL   Pete? Hi. Put out a "no comment." We're going to see what happens.

SCENE TEN

Russell's Hollywood apartment. His belongings are still in boxes. Russell runs in and finds his father, Stan holding a newspaper in his hand. Stan looks older and more defeated than he did in Russell's memory.

RUSSELL   Oh, Jesus, you . . . Dad! How did you get in?

STAN   The landlord let me . . . I wanted to see you, Rusty. I read this . . .

RUSSELL   Yeah, Dad, listen, that, that's not what it looks like. I . . .

STAN   My God, Rusty. My God. We thought you'd forgotten.

Russell freezes. He stares at Stan who is overcome with emotion. A long pause.

End of Act One

ACT II

Where we left off.

RUSSELL Forgotten? You thought I'd forgotten . . . what?

STAN (*Waving the newspaper*) This. Rusty, I'm so sorry. Do you have anything to drink?

RUSSELL What? I think, some bottled water. I finished the orange juice.

STAN That's all right. Do you have a glass?

RUSSELL They're still in a box. But I can . . .

STAN Never mind. (*He takes a flask from his pocket and takes a sip.*) You can understand. I'm still a bit shaken up.

RUSSELL Sure.

STAN You've spoken to your mother?

RUSSELL I just came from there.

STAN You were always thick as thieves. In spite of everything.

RUSSELL Everything?

STAN I left you alone. I figured, what can I do? I had other things . . . Aw, shit. I've been a terrible father. I have.

RUSSELL No, you haven't.

STAN Yes, I have. A complete flop. You have no idea how painful that is. To know you've failed your children.

RUSSELL Look, Dad, if you're fishing, stop it. Can we just get on with this?

STAN Don't talk that way to me. I'm your father, goddamn it.

RUSSELL I'm sorry.

STAN You give me that snitty graduate school attitude like I'm nothing to you . . .

RUSSELL I said I was sorry. Dad, please.

STAN Your mother must have had a conniption when she read this. Did she?

RUSSELL Yes.

STAN Good. Serves her right. It's about time it all caught up with her.

RUSSELL It's time *what* caught up with her?

STAN What she did. What you said.

RUSSELL I don't know what I said! I was making it up! It was all a goof, I swear to God.

STAN Well, you got it right. Every bit of it. You don't have to lie anymore. Your mother is a sick woman, Rusty. Always was. Always will be.

RUSSELL No. No, please. This isn't happening. This is insane.

STAN She hit you with an Emmy award. She absolutely did, just like you said. We had to get it replaced.

RUSSELL Oh, my God.

STAN Your science teacher, Mr. Fleming, started asking questions—why were you so moody in class? I had to meet with him, tell him everything was fine. Can you imagine how I felt?

RUSSELL   You remember Mr. Fleming?

STAN   Jesus. Why do you think Mrs. Kennedy stopped working for us?

RUSSELL   She got a better offer.

STAN   That's what we told you. You think someone could pay her more than we did? She couldn't stand to watch what was going on. She made a few remarks about "what makes a good mother" to Diane and then the shit hit the fan. She was crying when she left, afraid for you and Adam.

RUSSELL   Please, stop.

STAN   I'd see her get that restless look in her eye. And I knew what was coming. I'd see her walk up to your room . . .

RUSSELL   Well, why the fuck didn't you do something? I mean, Jesus Christ, you could have saved me from, from whatever it was you could have saved me from. What the hell was wrong with you?

STAN   I know, I know. Please, don't make this any worse for me than it already is.

RUSSELL   Worse for *you*?

STAN   I was weak, Rusty. I had no control over your mother. She's a monster. She thinks of no one but herself. You know that.

RUSSELL   No, I don't know.

STAN   Goddamn it, stop protecting her! She doesn't deserve it. Why do you think I'm in the sorry state I'm in now? It's all because of her. I've suffered, Russell. You have no idea.

RUSSELL   No, I guess I don't.

STAN That's because I never wanted to bother you. With all the sleepless nights I've spent going over it all in my mind . . .

RUSSELL You can't sleep?

STAN You've got your own life to worry about. You didn't need to hear about my pain. You didn't need to see your old man living in filth, fighting substance abuse. What could you have done?

RUSSELL Well, are you all right now? I mean, do you need any help?

Stan takes another sip from his flask.

STAN Now? Now I'm fine. I got my shit together now.

RUSSELL Well, good.

STAN I finally put it all behind me. I'm in a group. We talk. It's nice. I prayed you and your brother would never have to go through this, that somehow, you'd put it out of your mind. But I guess the truth comes back sooner or later.

RUSSELL What truth? Help me. Dad, I don't remember.

STAN Well, I do. I remember everything.

RUSSELL I feel dizzy.

Russell sits. Stan sits next to him and puts his arm on his shoulder.

STAN It's a lot to take in, kid. But now you know. The toothpaste is out of the tube. Things happened to you. Things that shouldn't happen to anyone, they happened to you. So, now what? Right? That's the hard part. Well, I'm here for you, Rusty. I know I wasn't around for a long time. I want to make up for that. Let's work together, you and me. We'll be a team, okay? And we'll take care of your mother. Don't you worry. We'll make her pay for what she's done.

SCENE TWO

Lights up on Linda Simmons. Music: Linda's sting.

LINDA Wednesday column. We had expected to hear vigorous denials from Diane Barrow. But so far, the star who's been accused of being another Mommie Dearest has left it at "no comment." Maybe that's because Barrow, who's always been one of our favorites, refuses to wallow in the muck of dirty laundry that seems to be everyone else's stock and trade these days. Still, things don't look too rosy for Diane. Her ex-husband and onetime producer, Stanley Burke, was seen yesterday at Fox, pitching his version of the story for a movie-of-the-week. Stay tuned.

Music: Linda's sting. Lights out on Linda and up on Russell and Pam at Java Nagila.

PAM This is a wonderful thing.

RUSSELL How can you say that?

PAM Do you realize what an opportunity this is for you? As a man? As an artist?

RUSSELL I'm listening.

PAM You must take this journey. Why do you think you started messing with this stuff in the first place? You think this is just some coincidence?

RUSSELL Where there's smoke?

PAM Something is forcing you to find the truth. Listen. That's your *muse*. You're going to do something important now. I can feel it. Just stop kvetching and focus.

RUSSELL You sound like my mother.

PAM Does she know about your dad?

RUSSELL (*Bitterly*) It was in the paper.

PAM What are you going to do?

RUSSELL I'm going to talk to her. See what she says.

PAM Are you sure? You really should check with Margaret. It's important not to confront your perpetrator before you're ready.

RUSSELL She's not "my perpetrator," she's my mother! She's not an archetype, not some phantom from the past, she's my mom.

PAM All I'm saying . . .

RUSSELL All you're saying is that I have to destroy my mother, my life, every happy memory of my childhood, and for what? Tell me, Pam! I have to sacrifice everything for what?

PAM For the truth. For the child you were.

RUSSELL Oh, no, please, please don't.

PAM For that little boy whose parents betrayed him. Who suffered pain and shame at the hand of the woman who was supposed to take care of him.

RUSSELL (*Breaking down despite himself, beginning to cry*) Please, stop. Please. Oh, God.

PAM I know it hurts. But you're not alone, you know?

Pam takes Russell in her arms.

RUSSELL   Why is this happening to me?

PAM   Why does it happen to anyone? No one knows. It's up to us to break the cycle. And you can help so much. There are so many in pain who don't have a voice. You can be that voice. Now you're one of us.

Russell pulls away from Pam, disturbed by her last comment. Pause.

RUSSELL   I want to see my mom.

PAM   Russell, please. Be careful.

SCENE THREE

Diane's home. The room is dark except for the flickering glare of a television. Diane watches a rerun of her show. She is drinking.

RUSSELL   My perpetrator.

DIANE   Well, Russell, this is a surprise. Aren't you afraid to be alone with me?

RUSSELL   I thought I'd risk it. What is this? You never drank. Only Dad drank.

DIANE   I drank with him sometimes.

RUSSELL   I don't remember that.

DIANE   No kidding.

RUSSELL   Do you always watch your show?

DIANE   Sometimes. When I need it.

RUSSELL   It's still really good. Everyone says so. It isn't dated at all.

DIANE   That's because it's never off the air.

RUSSELL   It's more than that. Your show had quality.

DIANE   Yes. It works. You could feel it at the time—the chemistry, the response, we were *up there*. So I watch and I remember. All those wonderful people. It was more than a show. They were my family. (*She picks up a remote control and turns off the TV.*)   So, you've spoken to your father. The Willy Loman of first-run syndication. What did he tell you?

RUSSELL   That I was right. It's true what the papers said.

DIANE   Do you believe him?

RUSSELL   I don't know. He cried. I never saw him do that before.

DIANE   You want me to cry? I can do it, I still have some Meisner training.

RUSSELL   Why would he lie?

DIANE   Oh, let's see. He hates me. He's a drunk having hallucinations. He's desperate for attention. He's looking for a TV deal. Pick one.

RUSSELL   Okay. He may be unstable, but he was very convincing.

DIANE   Your father could make himself believe anything. You know that. That's how you and Adam always got what you wanted. By the time you were eight years old, he was putty in your hands.

RUSSELL   That's not . . . oh, wait. I remember.

Stan appears. Russell speaks to him as a boy.

STAN What are we doing today, kiddo?

RUSSELL You said you would take me to Toys "R" Us to buy me electronic football.

STAN No I didn't. I don't remember that.

RUSSELL You did. Thursday night at dinner when we had lasagna. You said you'd take me to Toys "R" Us on Saturday to buy me electronic football because I did well on my report card. You promised.

STAN (*He tries to remember, then gives up.*) That's funny, I can't . . . oh, right, I remember! You got it, kiddo. Let's go.

RUSSELL Cool.

Stan exits.

DIANE I rest my case.

RUSSELL All right, but still . . . He remembered Mr. Fleming.

DIANE Who?

RUSSELL My science teacher. Dad said he had to lie to Mr. Fleming, to tell him I was all right.

DIANE Of course! He didn't want anyone knowing the truth. You were upset because your father was fucking every production assistant he could get his hands on. Mr. Fleming wouldn't be interested in that.

RUSSELL What?!

DIANE Your father couldn't keep his hands off anything with tits. Honestly. Why do you think Mrs. Kennedy left us?

RUSSELL She got a better offer?

DIANE   Please. She was tired of fighting him off. It was humiliating. How dare you take his side against me! How dare you!

RUSSELL   This isn't about taking sides, I'm just trying to make sense of this.

DIANE   Well, tough shit, you won't. This is life, Russell, it doesn't make sense.

RUSSELL   Mom, you're getting hysterical.

DIANE   It fell out of my hands! It was an accident and he still uses it to torture me, the bastard. I never meant it to hit you!

RUSSELL   What are you talking about?

DIANE   I hated going to the Emmys, I hated winning!

Lights change. Stan enters in a tuxedo, carrying an Emmy award. A moment later, Mrs. Kennedy enters.

STAN   So don't go anymore! See if I care.

DIANE   No, you wouldn't care at all. You could go without me and pick up some twenty-year-old prop girl from *All in the Family.*

STAN   Oh, we're back to this?

RUSSELL   Mom, Dad, please stop. Don't fight, come on.

STAN   Mrs. Kennedy, can you get him out of here?

MRS. KENNEDY   Russell, come on, go to bed now.

DIANE   Yeah, get him out of here before his father hits the bottle.

STAN   I'll hit you in a minute.

DIANE Oh, go ahead. Bite the hand that feeds you.

RUSSELL Mommy, please.

MRS. KENNEDY Russell, move it now.

STAN You know, you deserve that award, Diane. For a vicious bitch like you to become "America's Sweetheart," now that's some fucking performance.

Diane screams, "Asshole!" and throws the Emmy. Russell jumps up, crying, "Noooo." Stan and Mrs. Kennedy disappear into the wings. The lights change back.

DIANE It hit you. I would rather have ripped out my heart.

RUSSELL Was I hurt?

DIANE Not really. You got two stitches on your scalp. You can't even feel them I bet.

RUSSELL How did you know Dad brought that up?

DIANE I know him. He knows how to hurt me.

Russell sits down.

RUSSELL So that's it?

DIANE Of course. I'm so sorry. I figured you forgot about that night so I never talked about it. (*She sits next to Russell and holds him in her arms.*) How could I hurt you? I love you. You're my baby. We had a bond, you know we did. I spent every free minute in your room. You were my favorite.

RUSSELL I knew that.

DIANE You still are, my love. So? Let's call Pete. All right? We can call Helen too, get her started. You can talk to the

L.A. Times, Linda Simmons, *The Star* and *The Enquirer,* I don't care. But this thing's gone on long enough, don't you think?

Diane rises to retrieve her phone book. Pause.

RUSSELL   What did we do in my room?

DIANE   What?

RUSSELL   You spent all that time in my room. And except for one PTA night, I don't remember what we did.

DIANE   What are you implying?

RUSSELL   I don't know. I just feel compelled to ask.

DIANE   I'm losing my patience, Rusty. Are we going to call them now or not?

RUSSELL   It's a simple question. Clear, straightforward. What did we do in my room?

DIANE   We enjoyed each other. That's what we did.

RUSSELL   Did you touch me?

DIANE   Oh, for God's sake, Russell. You were my child. Of course I did.

RUSSELL   I don't mean it like that.

DIANE   Well, just how do you mean it? I breast-fed you as a baby. How about that? I didn't have to, not everybody did back then. And I liked it. It felt good. It gave me pleasure. Now, do you think that was wrong? Should I tear my hair out and do penance? What does your therapist say?

RUSSELL   How did we "enjoy each other"?

DIANE We played games. We laughed. I told you stories. What are you imagining?

RUSSELL I don't know. All that time in my room . . .

DIANE Stop! Stop it. I won't stand for this another minute. That's it. Get out, Russell. Get out of my house.

RUSSELL Please, just tell me.

DIANE Tell you what? What are you looking for? You want to say "Aha! That's why I'm so messed up. It was all her fault!" Well, I'm not going to help you with that one. Because, I hate to break this to you, kiddo, but you're not so bad. You're functioning, you look presentable, you're not drooling or wearing socks that don't match. You're intelligent, you have only slightly below average social skills. You're not begging for change and talking to yourself on La Cienega Boulevard. All in all, it seems I did pretty well considering what I had to work with. Now, if you're not happy with your life, well, that became exclusively your problem when you graduated from Beverly Hills High. Deal with it, Russell. You're okay.

RUSSELL I don't feel okay.

DIANE Tough. Go to a movie. Get laid. Be productive.

RUSSELL It's not that easy, Mom. I don't seem to have the tools. I never learned how to be happy. I never learned how to love. Somehow I'm always lost and alone.

DIANE And that's my fault? I never taught you how to be happy? How to love? Well, you're right. You caught me, I didn't. Because NO ONE KNOWS HOW TO BE HAPPY. NO ONE KNOWS HOW TO LOVE. Those things are hard, Russell. You gotta work day in, day out just to become deluded. I would teach you those things,

267

sweetheart, but God never gave me the lesson plan. You're on your own. Now, can we call them, for fuck's sake? My career is dying by the second.

RUSSELL I've got to think.

DIANE I see. So I just have to wait, is that it?

RUSSELL If you won't help me. I need to know how this got started. I need to know exactly what happened to me.

DIANE Oh, my poor baby. You'll never know that. You can lie on that couch till doomsday, but you'll never know. Not really. We can't go back. We're not allowed. The past doesn't wait for us, fixed, like some exhibit in a museum. We make it up every time ourselves. And nothing looks the same. What seemed so right at the time can suddenly look so wrong. There's no use taking a second look.

RUSSELL I need to figure things out.

DIANE Good luck. Let me know what happens. (*Russell turns to go.*) Wait. You came like that? It's cold out. You forget because it's California, but at night . . . Let me get you a jacket.

RUSSELL I don't need . . .

DIANE I'm getting you one.

Diane exits in search of a jacket.

SCENE FOUR

Margaret's office. Russell paces.

MARGARET She brought you a jacket.

RUSSELL One I left home a year ago. She'd had it dry-cleaned.

MARGARET   And you see this as a sign of . . .

RUSSELL   Pure maternal instinct. She wanted to make sure her child was warm and wouldn't catch cold. After the things I said to her, there was no reason for her to act that way.

MARGARET   "To *act* that way."

RUSSELL   Don't do that. All right? Please.

MARGARET   How are you feeling now?

RUSSELL   I feel horrible, what do you expect? I'm confused, terrified, exhausted. I've become rude to waiters—on those days I manage to leave my apartment, where my belongings still sit in cardboard boxes. I feel like a worthless piece of shit.

MARGARET   That's not necessarily your fault.

RUSSELL   No? Jesus, why is everyone so determined to let me off the hook?

MARGARET   Is that what you think I'm doing?

RUSSELL   No. I think you're trying to help me make sense of this.

MARGARET   Good.

RUSSELL   But life doesn't make sense. That's what my mother said.

MARGARET   She said that? Well, I suppose it may seem that way at times.

RUSSELL   But then you find the missing piece, and it all falls into place?

MARGARET   Sometimes.

RUSSELL   So you're like a detective. Is that it?

MARGARET   If you like.

RUSSELL   Well, I don't. "Detective" sounds scientific and you said this is an art. No, you're an artist. A creative genius.

MARGARET   Really?

RUSSELL   A storyteller. You're not looking for objective Truth, for who did what to whom. You're here to find the best story. The one that satisfies your audience.

MARGARET   The patient.

RUSSELL   Exactly.

MARGARET   This is very interesting.

RUSSELL   Oh, this is what I do best. (*He slips into graduate school mode.*)   You provide narrative. The close reading of the patient's life. You're the dramatist of our age. You come up with the denouement, the "What happened in Boston, Willy?" that explains why we've gone through so much pain. We come to you for what we're all searching for, our second act.

MARGARET   Yes, I see.

RUSSELL   It's like, old Aunt Loretta is a miserable bitch. No one knows why, until late in Act 2; we find out that Aunt Loretta lost her one true love in a boating accident and never got over it. Nice and tidy. Catharsis. Of course, Aunt Loretta may have been a miserable bitch anyway. Life may not really conform to the narrative, but we don't care. We all feel better now. And Aunt Loretta can go on *Oprah* and explain why it's not her fault she's a miserable bitch. Then we'll all be happy, when the world consists of nothing but a long row of chairs on a universal talk show. We can all point to the person next to us and say, "It's his fault."

MARGARET   Why are you here, Russell? Why did you come back?

RUSSELL   I want to hear my story. Maybe that's the way to handle this. Can I just think of what happened to me as a story? As a Shakespeare play I reread from time to time to glean life lessons, at a safe distance?

MARGARET   Possibly. Of course, that's charming if your story is *As You Like It*. But what if you lived through *Othello?* Or *Hamlet?*

RUSSELL   I never liked *Hamlet*. Not like you're supposed to. I just wanted him to act and face the inevitable. And now look at me. I've been visited by a ghost of my father who told me something rotten and I'm completely stymied.

Russell sits and rubs his forehead, harder and harder. Pause.

MARGARET   Russell?

RUSSELL   I'm having some real problems here. I think I better do something.

MARGARET (*Concerned, urgent*)   All right. Russell, if you agree, I'd like us to start meeting every day. Also, there are some other options you should be aware of. We can begin to experiment with hypnosis and sodium amytal, which is a kind of truth serum. These techniques don't work for everyone, but when they do, we see dramatic results.

RUSSELL   We must be in Act 2.

Lights up on Linda Simmons. Music: Linda's sting.

LINDA Wednesday column. This is a dark time for Diane Barrow. We haven't heard a word from her since those stunning accusations that have kept tongues wagging over the artichoke risotto at Orso. And now, Kirby Phillips, the adorable child actor who played Barrow's son years ago has come forward, claiming that Diane molested him repeatedly in his trailer before tapings of the classic series. Phillips, who is currently on probation for robbing four convenience stores at gunpoint, tearfully recounts his experience this week in three exclusive tell-all interviews.

 With all these developments, one can't help but wonder, were we wrong when we immediately rallied to Diane's side? Were there warning signs that we simply overlooked? I had lunch not long ago with Diane in New York. And though I didn't write so at the time, I was alarmed by her behavior. She was emotional, manic, and secretive to the point that she smashed the tape I made of the interview on the table in front of me. Did she know then that her world was about to come crashing down around her? Most disturbing of all, I keep remembering the way her eyes lit up when I asked about her new beau. "He's younger," she said, "much younger." The wicked smile on her face when she uttered those words now haunts me every night. Of course, Barrow is innocent until proven guilty. And there are no criminal proceedings against her. Yet.

Music: Linda's sting. Lights out on Linda. Lights up on Diane at home with Paul. She's just read the column.

DIANE He was a nasty little kid. He could never remember his lines, he terrorized the crew. Even then we used to say he'd end up in jail or running a network.

PAUL   Rotten little punk.

DIANE   I couldn't stand him. And I felt guilty about it—the idea of hating a ten-year-old. Isn't that awful? Well, I don't feel guilty anymore.

PAUL   He has no credibility. No one will take this seriously. At least, no one you'd want anything to do with.

Taylor enters.

DIANE   Hello, my love.

TAYLOR   Hi.

PAUL   I'll just . . . I'll keep going through the mail.

Paul exits.

DIANE   Have you read the latest?

TAYLOR   I got the usual calls. Only this time they asked me questions. Sick questions about us.

DIANE   I'm sorry.

TAYLOR   Diane, I've been thinking . . .

DIANE   Oh. I see . . .

TAYLOR   No, you don't.

DIANE   This is all too much for you, clearly . . .

TAYLOR   It's not what you think.

DIANE   No? Then tell me, what?

TAYLOR   I want to do the right thing. I'm standing by you and I want everyone in the world to know it. Di, (*He takes a deep breath and gets down on one knee.*)   will you marry me?

DIANE Oh, Taylor. That is easily the kindest thing anyone's ever done for me. You're a good, decent man. You're as gorgeous inside as you are outside and that almost never happens. I love you. But I won't marry you.

TAYLOR Please. I've thought a lot about this.

DIANE I'm sure you have. But I'm afraid the answer has to be no.

TAYLOR But why? If you love me, why not?

DIANE Because you don't want me to marry you. Not really.

TAYLOR Yes, I do. Now you're treating me like a child.

DIANE I'm only speaking the simple truth. Nothing would last between us and deep down you know that. Today or tomorrow, you'll give me up for someone younger and more beautiful.

TAYLOR I love you.

DIANE And I love you. Still, that day will come, sooner than we expect . . .

TAYLOR Stop it, stop saying that. All my life, people have been underestimating me because of the way I look, because, I don't know, because I'm a simple guy. What do I have to do to prove myself?

DIANE Marry an older woman in trouble?

TAYLOR Fine. Are you trying to get rid of me with insults?

DIANE I want to make this easy for both of us. I don't think we should see each other anymore. Let's call it quits.

TAYLOR How can you do this to me?

DIANE Go, Taylor.

TAYLOR But . . .

DIANE Please. I can't comfort you now. I don't have the strength. Just go. (*Taylor turns to go.*)   Wait! Can I at least have a kiss?

He goes to her and kisses her. Diane pulls away first. She fixes his hair and pushes him gently away. He turns to leave but then stops.

TAYLOR When you said no, I felt relieved. Does that make me a horrible person?

DIANE No. Telling me makes you a horrible person. (*They share a light laugh.*)   Remember me fondly. No matter what you hear.

TAYLOR No matter what.

Taylor exits. Paul reenters, quietly.

PAUL Are you all right? (*Diane shakes her head.*)   Do you want to tell me about it?

DIANE Weren't you listening?

PAUL No. I could hear a little.

DIANE Good. Then I'd rather not talk about it.

PAUL Diane? This letter came. I know this isn't a good time but I couldn't for the life of me figure out when a good time would be. It's from Adam.

Diane takes the letter from him and begins to read. ADAM BURKE, *a more relaxed, nerdier version of Russell, appears behind her and speaks the letter.*

ADAM Dear Mom, It's funny. I was about to call you with happy news. Sarah's pregnant. I know you're probably pissed off at the idea of becoming a grandmother but you knew it had to happen sometime. Anyway, we're very excited about it.

I don't know what to think about all this stuff in the paper. Reporters keep calling the house but we just hang up the phone. We're getting a new number soon. It's been pretty unnerving.

I don't remember any of the stuff they're talking about. Not even a little bit. But I've seen on TV that doesn't mean much. I know it's possible that I've just forgotten, that my brain crashed or something (sorry about the computer term).

I still love you, Mom, and I feel really confused about all this. Still, Sarah and I have talked about it and we've decided that maybe it would be better if you didn't come to visit once the baby is born. At least not right away. I'm asking Russell the same thing. I'm sure you understand, this being our first kid and everything. We don't want to take any unnecessary risks. We also know that these things can repeat themselves, so I'm going to talk to someone. (Don't worry, I'll keep it out of the papers. How could Russell be so stupid?) I guess we'll keep a close eye on me too.

I hope you're okay. I really do. Work is good.

Love, Adam.

Lights out on Adam. Diane puts down the letter.

DIANE When things turn against you, is there anyone you can appeal to? To say, "That's enough?" God or someone?

PAUL You just have to hold on tight and ride it out.

Diane rises. She speaks haltingly, utterly lost.

DIANE I need something. Call . . . call . . .

PAUL Your lawyer? Helen?

DIANE Doctor Weisman. I need something. Call the doctor.

Russell's apartment. There's a knock on the door. Stan calls from outside.

STAN   Russell! Russell, it's your father. Open up for God's sake! You want me to call the cops? I'm in no mood for an overdose situation so don't even think about it!

Russell enters and goes to open the door. Stan enters with a paper bag. He is sharply dressed.

STAN (*cont.*)   Look at me, Russell, I want to talk to you. Jesus, you look like shit.

RUSSELL   Jesus, you look *great*.

STAN   I had a meeting. (*He hands him the bag.*)   Here, I bought you some juice . . . I figured I drank yours . . .

RUSSELL   You didn't, but thanks. That's sweet.

STAN   You gave me some scare. Why don't you answer your phone?

RUSSELL   Too many people calling.

STAN   Reporters?

RUSSELL   Total strangers. Someone posted my number on a Web site, so all these wackos are offering their support.

STAN   They care about you.

RUSSELL   They never did before. I've been going to the same car wash since high school, I never knew the guy at the register was molested by his babysitter. Now I know.

STAN   You see how powerful this is?

RUSSELL   Where am I going to wash my car?

STAN So, what, you just sit around in your bathrobe all day?

RUSSELL I go to therapy. They're giving me this drug. It's supposed to help me remember, but, so far, it just makes me groggy.

STAN Well, keep at it. You'll come up with something, believe me.

RUSSELL What's the rush?

STAN No rush. I just don't want you to lose this momentum. That's why I'm here, actually. Get dressed, we've got an appointment.

RUSSELL What? With who?

STAN Someone who can help. I'll explain in the car. Have you had lunch? How about we eat, then I'll buy you some clothes, like old times.

RUSSELL Dad, stop. Where are you taking me?

STAN We're going to meet a lawyer.

RUSSELL Oh, no we're not.

STAN Now don't, don't . . . Shirley, from my group, gave me this guy's name. She had tears in her eyes, said he saved her life. He specializes in this kind of case.

RUSSELL You expect me to press charges?

STAN I know, it sounds horrible. But don't reject things out of hand. It's the only way to get closure, Rusty. For both of us. I've spoken to people all over town and they all agree, that's what we're missing.

RUSSELL Missing? What are you talking about?

STAN Okay, hear me out. As you know, I've been looking for an opportunity to tell your story to the world in a meaningful way.

RUSSELL You made the deal at Fox.

STAN Almost. Now, I know what you're thinking, but these people, they've got a lot of sense, they're good with story. And they all said, we've got no third act—well, on TV they work in seven acts but we were using the standard three-act model in terms of . . .

RUSSELL The point?

STAN We don't have an ending. And, you know, when they said that, it hit me like a shot. Because I took one of those story structure seminars—have you ever gone?

RUSSELL No.

STAN Oh, you gotta, it's fabulous, it changes the way you look at . . . life, everything. See, now look at yourself sitting there in your bathrobe: You're a wreck, at your lowest point. End of Act Two. Right? How do you get back on top? By finding your inner strength and fighting! By punishing the bad guys and riding off down Sunset. That's our ending.

RUSSELL You want me to put Mom in jail so you'll have a climax for your TV Movie?

STAN Of course not. This is about you, triumphing over adversity and pain. Anything else is a bonus, on the back end, after the trial. Although, I won't lie to you—if this plays out the way I think it will, this could be a feature.

RUSSELL Great. Maybe I could dish up some dirt on you, too. Then we'd have a sequel.

STAN That's not funny.

RUSSELL You have any other vendettas? This could be a franchise.

STAN Look, if you're not going to take this seriously . . .

RUSSELL Good-bye, Dad. Thanks for the juice.

Beat. Stan angrily heads to the door.

STAN All right, fine. I tried to help but you shut me out. The hell with it. You do what you want. Drop out, same as always.

RUSSELL That's not fair!

STAN Isn't it? Russell, I know. That's why I kept my distance all this time. I couldn't bear watching you fall into the same rut—spinning your wheels, invisible, hearing people forget your last name. This isn't revenge. It's my last chance to push you out of her shadow, once and for all. Let me help you find your light. Follow this through and let the chips fall where they may. You do that, and I promise, Russell Burke, the world will see you now.

Scene Seven

Diane's home. Diane shows in Pam.

PAM Thank you so much for seeing me.

DIANE Well, why not? I can't go out now, I'm a prisoner in my own home.

PAM I'm sorry.

DIANE And I was glad you called. Not too many people are calling now.

PAM   I guess it's times like these you find out who your friends are.

DIANE   "Times like these?" CNN is running clips of me kissing little Kirby every ten minutes with experts pointing out evidence of my perversion. Some psychiatrist was on *The Today Show* advising parents how to talk to their children about me. The *New Yorker* calls my disgrace "the final unmasking of the sitcom mother paradigm"—whatever the fuck that means. You're very young, sweetheart. I've been through a lot, and let me tell you, there are no times like these.

PAM   Then why haven't you done anything about it?

DIANE   What?

PAM   "No comment." Not one interview. Not one sound bite.

DIANE   What would be the use? No one would believe me.

PAM   Is that the reason?

DIANE   What else could it be?

PAM   Something is holding you back.

DIANE   (*Dry*)   Not my conscience.

PAM   No. Your sense of occasion.

Beat.

DIANE   Go on.

PAM   You know how important this is. Situations like this don't just create themselves.

DIANE   You think I'm guilty.

PAM I didn't say that.

DIANE You think Russell is right to torture me.

PAM That's not what he's doing. Russell is on a quest, *the* quest, for self. What is identity if not the sum of our experiences? Russell wants to find out who he is. Maybe it's time for you to do the same. If it's necessary to suffer now, suffer. If there are sins to atone for, atone. You've kept your silence, I know it, because you need to fully have this experience. Because, in spite of everything, Ms. Barrow, you are a great woman.

DIANE Please. Call me Diane.

Lights out on Pam and Diane and up on the other side of the stage to reveal Paul and Russell meeting for lunch at the food court at the Century City Mall. They both have trays of food.

PAUL What did you get?

RUSSELL A burger. You?

PAUL Tandoori. I hope the food court is all right.

RUSSELL Sure. Feels like the right place to eat nowadays, when it's wrong to assume that any two people might enjoy eating the same food.

PAUL Sooooooo, how are you?

RUSSELL Wow, Paul, you make a lousy spy. I can't believe she put you up to this.

PAUL She didn't. Your mother has no idea, honest. I just . . . I feel very strongly about what's happening. There are rumors you're going to file charges.

RUSSELL Where did you hear that?

PAUL   I saw your father on *Hard Copy*.

RUSSELL   Well, he's a little premature. I'm not yet convinced that the next step toward happiness is sending my mom to the big house.

PAUL   You're in a tough spot.

RUSSELL   You have no idea.

PAUL   Yes, I do. Russell, there's something I have to tell you. I was abused.

RUSSELL   My God. Why is it everybody I meet now has some terrible story?

PAUL   Probably because almost everybody does.

Lights up on Diane and Pam, out on Russell and Paul.

DIANE   You are wise beyond your years. How do you know so much?

PAM   Simple. I've been through a lot. I was abused.

DIANE   I'm sorry.

PAM   I'll tell you my story.

Lights up on Paul and Russell, out on Diane and Pam.

PAUL   I'll tell you my story, if you like.

RUSSELL   You don't have to.

PAUL   It's important for us to share these things. My father is a cop. A cop, can you imagine? Let's just say I was not his favorite.

RUSSELL   I'm sorry.

PAUL I haven't gotten to the bad part. Enter Mr. Wilcox. He ran the evening activity center at our church. He was a "community leader," my mother always said. Mr. Wilcox started coming round when I was twelve. Sometimes he kept me in his car, sometimes he took me to where he lived. Sometimes four or five times a week. At first, I didn't mind, it got me out of the house. But then I did mind. I was ashamed, I was bewildered. Worst of all, I was aroused. When it ended, I was still afraid. Afraid I'd become like him. And that fear never goes away.

RUSSELL Where is Mr. Wilcox now?

PAUL In prison. I had to. He was doing it again. To others.

RUSSELL Did you forget?

PAUL Never.

RUSSELL But you think it's possible that I did?

PAUL Maybe. Freud thought so. What's too painful to remember, we simply choose to forget.

RUSSELL That's not Freud.

PAUL No. It's Alan and Marilyn Bergman, who are far more reliable.

Lights up on Diane and Pam, out on Russell and Paul. Pam has told her story.

DIANE Where is Marty now?

PAM Marty died in a car accident coming home drunk from a gig in Philadelphia.

DIANE Good. The bastard. What an awful story. You poor thing.

PAM Thank you. Oh, God . . . You don't know what this feels like. To tell you these things. To hear you say that . . . (*Pam is overcome with emotion. Diane is uncomfortable.*) It's like a dream. All that time, when I was so unhappy, I would watch your show and think about you. You were so sensible and loving . . . I'd pretend that you were going to walk into our living room any minute and make everything all right. I just wanted you to see me, to know about me. To stroke my hair and say, "You poor thing." And now, here you are . . .

Pam puts her head on Diane's lap and holds her by the waist. Diane is bewildered. She strokes Pam's hair.

DIANE Poor thing. How strange. We argued with the network over whether or not Diane Rogers should even have children. I was against it. I was afraid I wouldn't look comfortable in the role. But I guess I pulled it off.

PAM You have no idea, do you? How much you mean to us.

DIANE No, I guess I don't. All you mixed-up children. What do you want from me? What can I do?

PAM Tell the truth.

Lights up on Russell and Paul, out on Diane and Pam.

RUSSELL She'll deny it to her grave.

PAUL She may not remember fully herself.

RUSSELL Oh, come on. Say some truly awful things occurred, do you think it's possible to ignore something that obvious?

PAUL One word. Liberace.

RUSSELL That's not the same thing.

PAUL Of course it is. Little blue-haired ladies would go and see this lurid queen in rhinestones by the busload the same week they'd kick their faggot children out of the house. Denial is an amazing thing.

RUSSELL And the only way for us to stop it is to fight for the Truth, right wrongs. You think I should put my mother in jail.

PAUL Russell, I've told you all this so you would know I don't come to this lightly. I've been through a lot, so I hope you'll listen to me when I tell you: Drop it.

RUSSELL Excuse me?

PAUL Let it go.

RUSSELL I can't believe you're saying that.

PAUL I'm sort of surprised myself.

RUSSELL After what you did to Mr. Wilcox . . .

PAUL Mr. Wilcox was hanging around playgrounds. Your mother is not that kind of threat.

RUSSELL Does that excuse whatever happened?

PAUL Of course not. But punishing her is not important. You need to work this through and get your life together. But let your mother be.

RUSSELL You really do care about her, don't you?

PAUL Not the way you think. Not as a friend, or some kooky woman I work with.

RUSSELL Then how do you think of her?

PAUL (*Firm, with deep conviction*) As a star. Russell, your mother's a star and that fact shouldn't be forgotten. You wouldn't be hurting just her, you'd be hurting everyone.

RUSSELL But what about exposing hypocrisy? Revealing the painful truth to people in denial?

PAUL I know, I know. But she's a star. What can I say? She's a rare creature and I for one would hate to give that up. Let me tell you something about Judy Garland . . . (*Off Russell's smirk.*) Yes, yes, a gay man who loves Judy Garland, what a cliché. Well, fuck you, she's fabulous. Anyway, there's this tape. A videotape of Judy rehearsing for an appearance that evening on the Hollywood Palace. Some sick cameraman kept it and made copies so now every queen, including myself, has it as a keepsake. It's near "the end." Judy looks like she just woke up from a nap. Her hair is all *skwooshed* to one side. No makeup. She's wearing black pedal pushers and a turtleneck with the sleeves rolled up. There are dark bruises up and down her arms. It's a wonder she's standing at all. She sings, "What the World Needs Now Is Love Sweet Love," completely wrong for her and a terrible song. There is no interpretation, no soul, just the notes. In the middle, she forgets the words. And as you watch this tape, you feel as if you are looking into the deepest, darkest corners of her despair. The tragedy that she became, that had always been just beneath the surface where it belonged, is now front and center. And as you watch, you know this was something you weren't meant to see.

RUSSELL It destroys the illusion.

PAUL It destroys *her*. Don't tell me her talent and beauty were any less real than her pain. They were linked. Yes, it would have been wonderful if someone had interfered and said, "My God, Judy, you're killing yourself," and saved her life. But no one did. All that is *past*. Why let her dark side, which had to be there, obliterate her magic? I would be so happy if I could erase the memory of that scene forever. Don't do that to Diane Barrow. Let us have her.

SCENE EIGHT

Helen Menken's office. Helen talks on the phone through a headset. Diane waits for her.

HELEN   Yes, I'm in contact with her. No. No charges have been filed, as far as we know. Look, I'm working on her, what else can I do? I'll keep you posted. All right, kid. (*She checks notes on a Rolodex card.*)   Love to . . . Marilyn and the twins. (*She presses a button and addresses Diane.*)   I don't understand you, I really don't.

DIANE   I'm enigmatic.

HELEN   For months, I'm listening to you chew my head off— get me on TV, get me back in the spotlight. That's what you wanted.

DIANE   Not like this.

HELEN   One rarely gets to choose. Everyone's asking me, why won't she talk? Why the hell doesn't she defend herself? Unless, of course, she did it. (*Off Diane's cryptic stare.*)   That's what they say. And it pains me to hear it. I'd rather cut off my ears and feed them to dogs, I mean it. Personally, I don't believe that good-for-nothing kid of yours. He looked creepy at the Emmys. We all said so.

DIANE   Oh, Helen, shut up, will you?

HELEN   That's how you speak to me? I'm the one standing by you. I'm trying to revive your career.

DIANE What career? I say I'm an actress but who am I fooling? I haven't worked in ages. And I don't deserve to. I have no discipline, no technique.

HELEN Diane, sweetheart, I've worked in this business for forty years and believe me, that doesn't matter.

DIANE Well, it should. You wouldn't be reviving a career, you'd be selling a ghost. A tainted memory of somebody appealing. A cheap memento. Like one of those plates they sell from the Franklin Mint.

HELEN Look, I don't mind listening to creative people bitch and moan with self-pity. That's part of my job and I take my job seriously. But every once in a while, I have to stand up and say, "Jesus, lady, enough already." You're afraid you're not what you were twenty years ago? Well, nobody is. And maybe twenty years ago you weren't so hot either.

DIANE Is this your idea of support?

HELEN You don't need support, you need a good swift kick in the ass. It doesn't matter what you were then. You've got to realize who you are now. And whether you like what you find or not, I've got people calling me all day begging for it. This is a buyers' market, Diane. And Pete and I don't like telling every publisher, every network, and Barbara Walters that you're not interested.

DIANE (*She sees the irony*) Barbara Walters? She called?

HELEN She wants a full hour. Nobody but you. But we said no. After all, we can't let her interview an "enigmatic plate." (*She sees a light on her phone.*) Oh, shit, I've been waiting for this call. Stay right there. (*She presses a button.*) Barry? Yeah, he read the script and he's interested, with minor reservations. He wants to throw out the first forty pages. He wants a new beginning. Don't tell me it can't be done. Look, if you have to make revisions, you'll do it. Or you'll lose the whole thing. (*Diane listens, then grabs her things and waves to Helen.*) Wait, hold on. Diane, where are you going?

DIANE I know what to do.

SCENE NINE

Russell's apartment. Russell sleeps. Mrs. Kennedy appears.

MRS. KENNEDY Russell? Russell, wake up, child, I haven't got all night.

RUSSELL Mrs. Kennedy? Oh, my God, Mrs. Kennedy!

MRS. KENNEDY This apartment is filthy.

RUSSELL Well, I haven't really unpacked.

MRS. KENNEDY You never did pick up after yourself.

RUSSELL Wait, you can't really be here. I'm dreaming. Is that it? This is a dream, right?

MRS. KENNEDY Whatever.

RUSSELL But why would I dream about you? Oh! Interpretive mode. The answers are in the margins. You're a marginal figure in my life, so there must be some significance . . .

MRS. KENNEDY My Lord, don't you ever stop talking? You're asleep, Rusty, so shut up.

RUSSELL Yes, ma'am.

MRS. KENNEDY   And I don't appreciate being called a marginal figure. I spent more hours than I wish to remember taking care of you boys.

RUSSELL   I just meant . . .

MRS. KENNEDY   I had a whole life you don't know shit about. A life that doesn't fit in anybody's margins. I had a hard life and a difficult death. So have some respect.

RUSSELL   I'm sorry. Mrs. Kennedy, I'm so confused. Everyone's waiting for me to remember. You were there! Tell me, please, what happened?

MRS. KENNEDY   Oh, no. You can't get out of it that easy.

RUSSELL   You won't tell me? That's not fair!

MRS. KENNEDY   Fair? This life ain't fair, Rusty. Was it fair that I spent my time making sandwiches for you? How come nobody was cooking for me?

RUSSELL   I thought you liked taking care of me.

MRS. KENNEDY   If that's the way you remember it.

RUSSELL   Oh, God. So it was worse than I thought.

MRS. KENNEDY   There you go, being all dramatic. You're your mother's child, that's for sure. Russell, do you know what *tsuris* is?

RUSSELL   I think so. It's Yiddish. It means "problems."

MRS. KENNEDY   Worse than just problems, it means what is bringing your life *down*.

RUSSELL   How do you know that?

MRS. KENNEDY   After I left your family, I worked for this nice Jewish woman, Mrs. Scheinbaum. Her kids were all grown up so she liked to sit in the kitchen with me while her husband was at work at one of the studios. And I'd tell her all about how Billy, my son, almost got shot on his way home from school, and how my sister's husband beat her up real bad.

RUSSELL   I didn't know you had a son.

MRS. KENNEDY   Well, Mrs. Scheinbaum, she would just shake her head and say, "You think *you've* got *tsuris!*"

RUSSELL   How insulting.

MRS. KENNEDY   I didn't take it that way. Mrs. Scheinbaum, she told me this old saying. She said, "If you walked into a room filled with shelves and shelves of everybody's *tsuris,* you'd still pick your own."

RUSSELL   Is that supposed to be comforting? That my problems aren't as bad as other people's?

MRS. KENNEDY   Sometimes, that's all we have.

She starts to leave.

RUSSELL   But that's not even true. What about people lying in the street? Or the Holocaust?

MRS. KENNEDY   How should I know? I'm just a marginal figure.

RUSSELL   Mrs. Kennedy? I'm sorry I didn't know you better.

MRS. KENNEDY   (*She turns back to him*)   You should be. Frankie, my husband, used to say I was a good woman. I came from nothing, worked hard, and I lived with a TV star for a while. Not too bad. I made my own story, Russell. That's what a person's got to do. And if you don't like the first few chapters, throw 'em out.

RUSSELL Wait, wait! Mrs. Kennedy, I forgot to ask you! Why did you leave us?

MRS. KENNEDY Who remembers?

And she's gone.

RUSSELL No, wait!

SCENE TEN

Diane's home. Diane, in a conservative suit, considers accessories. Paul enters.

PAUL The flowers and the food arrived, so everything's under control. And it looks like the weather's clearing up so you should have a nice shot . . .

DIANE *(Holding out two scarves)* What do you think?

PAUL Either one.

DIANE Okay.

PAUL But the beige is better.

DIANE Paul? Am I doing the right thing?

PAUL I don't know. But wear the beige.

Russell enters.

RUSSELL Mom? What's going on down there?

DIANE Russell, what are you doing here? This isn't a good time . . .

RUSSELL I wanted to see you. I think we should talk.

DIANE Well, I can't now, I'm very busy.

RUSSELL   Why? What's going on?

Diane looks to Paul who clearly wants to tell.

DIANE   All right, Paul, tell him.

PAUL   Barbara Walters is coming.

RUSSELL   Oh. Wow. I didn't know.

PAUL   But not for a little while. So you two relax. I'll take care of everything.

Paul looks at both of them, takes the other scarf from Diane, and exits.

RUSSELL   You look great, Mom.

DIANE   Thank you.

RUSSELL   I'm glad to see you looking so well. The last time I was here . . .

DIANE   I was very angry.

RUSSELL   I don't blame you. This must have been rough for you.

DIANE   It was. Dr. Weisman gave me some pills . . .

RUSSELL   Oh, God . . .

DIANE   Then it got better. There's something pure and liberating in public humiliation. You realize who you are. I have to get ready.

RUSSELL   I know you do. (*Diane sits and prepares for her interview.*)   I saw Mrs. Kennedy.

DIANE   What?

RUSSELL   In a dream.

DIANE   Oh.

RUSSELL   And I remembered it. I remembered my dream.

DIANE   That's good.

RUSSELL   It was good to see her.

DIANE   Did she say anything interesting?

RUSSELL   No, not really.

DIANE   That's her.

RUSSELL   She helped me remember something.

DIANE   What now?

RUSSELL   She said something. She said, "You're your mother's child, that's for sure." I knew I'd heard that before. And then it hit me. That's what she said when I punched out Kirby Phillips.

DIANE   What?

RUSSELL   I was six or seven. I came to visit you at the studio. I liked to sit in your dressing room and listen to you run lines. Do you remember?

DIANE   Of course I do. If you didn't laugh, I'd fire another writer.

RUSSELL   Well, one day, Mrs. Kennedy took me after school. And when I got there I saw you and Kirby on the set. He was doing some stupid dance and singing a song. You were smiling at him, so proud. Like he was your own son. And for a second, I couldn't breathe.

DIANE   I never liked him, you have to believe me.

RUSSELL   I knew it was just an act. But that didn't make it any better. So later, I cornered Kirby behind one of the trailers. I grabbed him and said, "You get this straight. She's my mother. She's not yours and she never will be. She's mine!" And then I punched him as hard as I could, right in the stomach. That's when Mrs. Kennedy found us and dragged me kicking and screaming to the car. "You're your mother's child, that's for sure."

DIANE Poor Kirby.

RUSSELL It was the cruelest thing I've ever done. No wonder he's a derelict. But I was afraid he'd take you away from me. And I couldn't let that happen. I knew something then. Something I managed to forget along the way—I need you.

Diane has finished her preparations.

DIANE What are you saying?

RUSSELL All these years, I've been so afraid of being *just* your son, as if it were some kind of curse. But it was okay back then, when I beat up Kirby Phillips to make sure no one took my place. What's wrong with being just your son now?

DIANE You're more than that.

RUSSELL Not yet. I was too busy running from you to become anything myself. Maybe now I will. In the meantime, I've made a decision. I'm letting it go. Whatever you did to me, whatever we did to each other, my statute of limitations is up. From now on, my life is my problem. You're off the hook.

DIANE But don't you want to know what happened?

RUSSELL No. Not really. Because whatever it was, it didn't make me who I am, I'm sure of it. Besides, as far as I'm concerned, I was happy then—happy in a way I haven't been since. Back in those easy, glistening days when I was just your son, and we were filled with joy. Do you know what I mean?

DIANE Yes, I do.

RUSSELL I had a feeling you would.

DIANE What will you do?

RUSSELL I don't know. I'll go my way and be an ordinary, unhappy person. Maybe I'll be lucky and become deluded.

DIANE What about your peace of mind?

RUSSELL I'd rather have you. I want my mommy—the beautiful and scary Diane Barrow.

DIANE (*She begins to cry*) I wasn't expecting this. Life is so full of surprises all of a sudden. I wonder why that is.

RUSSELL Oh, Mom, don't cry.

DIANE Let me cry. I need it.

RUSSELL No, don't. Save it for Barbara.

Diane laughs and hugs him close.

DIANE Oh, Russell, I've missed you so much. But now you're back. Look at you, you're back and we're together. And I can help you.

RUSSELL You can?

DIANE Yes. I can teach you. I can teach you what you need most of all.

RUSSELL And what is that?

DIANE How to go on. That's what you want, isn't it? Well, that's my specialty. How to keep going. Even when it feels like your best days are behind you.

Paul enters, having seen the face of God.

PAUL   She's here.

DIANE   I'll be right down. (*Paul exits.*)   How do I look?

RUSSELL   Incredible. It's too bad.

DIANE   What is?

RUSSELL   I ruined the interview. Barbara will be so disappointed when you tell her it was all a big mistake.

DIANE   But it wasn't.

RUSSELL   What?

DIANE   Oh, damn. I wanted Margaret to be here when I told you.

RUSSELL   You spoke to Dr. Thurm?

DIANE   Sweetheart, I have so much to thank you for, not just today. You forced me to take a good hard look at things. Things I didn't want to see. Starting with my childhood. Things happened to me . . .

RUSSELL   Oh, no. Mom, please don't. Don't do this . . .

DIANE   Russell, listen to me. We'll do what we have to do to put this all behind us. All right? *I'll show you.*

RUSSELL   So then it's true?

A long beat. Diane looks at him with great love and regret.

DIANE   It's true enough.

Coda: music: Linda's sting, then Mozart's Elvira Madigan Piano Concerto. *The rest of the action is free of specific location. The other characters appear when they speak and exit when they finish.*

LINDA Monday column. Who would have predicted the incredible comeback of Diane Barrow? It was only a year ago that those stunning accusations of child abuse dealt her reputation a knock-down blow. But this star refused to go down for the count. Diane showed courage and grace unheard of in Hollywood and came forward to reveal her own troubled past.

DIANE At first, I was terrified. But the flood of support from fans and loved ones convinced me I was doing the right thing. Even Kirby Phillips, my darling costar from years ago, gave me his forgiveness and blessing.

MARGARET When she called, I was reluctant, of course. But just look at her now.

DIANE You know, Linda, I'm a grandmother now. And when I think that telling my story may make this world a safer place for little David . . . God, I feel good inside.

PAM At last, we have found our voice.

LINDA Shedding her glamorous image and wearing no makeup, Diane wowed critics and audiences alike in the bold TV movie based on her best-selling book, *Breaking the Cycle: The Diane Barrow Story* in which she played her own mother as well as herself. Insiders say the star should make room for that third Emmy.

DIANE I'm just so proud of this work.

LINDA And she should be. The movie scored big in sweeps weeks and blew the Fox version supervised by Diane's ex-husband out of the water and off the schedule.

STAN It never ends. But don't worry about me. I've got a lot of irons in the fire.

LINDA And you can expect a nomination for Taylor McDonald, the sexy young actor who was so moving as Diane's tormented son, Russell. Those two have been seen dining at hot spots around town but Taylor says . . .

TAYLOR We're just good friends.

LINDA Maybe. But they're teaming up again this fall. Superagent Helen Menken has put together the deal for Diane's eagerly anticipated remake of *Mildred Pierce*.

DIANE This won't be some stale retread of a classic. We've got lots of surprises.

PAUL "I can't believe it! My mother, a waitress!"

LINDA And what of the real-life Russell, whose personal struggle sent his mother on this painful journey of discovery?

RUSSELL I've started a theater company. I'm directing my own version of *The Seagull*. *Constantine Lives*. It works.

LINDA The future looks bright for this fine young man and his marvelous mother—truly a star for our times.

Music: Linda's sting. All exit except Diane and Russell.

DIANE Russell? (*He turns to face her. Music:* The Diane Barrow Show *theme song played softly on a piano.*) There's my beautiful . . . (*She catches herself.*) There's my son. We came through.

RUSSELL Yes we did.

DIANE I always knew, somehow we'd find each other again.

RUSSELL Mom? I met a girl. She helped me unpack.

DIANE Well . . . good. I'm glad.

RUSSELL   Thank you.

DIANE   So. I guess you've finished. You've figured things out.

RUSSELL   No. But that's all right. I'll watch what I do next.

Russell kisses his mother on the forehead. Taylor appears upstage. Diane goes to him and takes his hand. She turns and gives Russell a Diane Rogers wave. He smiles at her. The lights fade.

END OF PLAY